Mark's Holy Adventure:
Preaching Mark's Gospel for Year B

Bruce G. Epperly

D1452087

Parson's Porch Books

Mark's Holy Adventure: Preaching Mark's Gospel for Year B

ISBN: Softcover 978-1-951472-92-4

Copyright © 2014 by Bruce G. Epperly

To order additional copies of this book, contact:

Parson's Porch Books
1-423-475-7308
www.parsonsporch.com

Parson's Porch Books is an imprint of Parson's Porch & Company (PP&C) in Cleveland, Tennessee. PP&C is an innovative non-profit organization which raises money by publishing books of noted authors, representing all genres. All donations from contributors and profits from publishing are shared with the poor.

CONTENTS

WORDS OF THANKS

Every project is a team effort. No doubt the writing of Mark's Gospel was the result of many storytellers and a few writers before the emergence of the final text attributed to an unknown "Mark." This is certainly true of this lectionary commentary. I give thanks for my parents, Everett and Loretta Epperly, from whom I learned to love scripture and One whose love gave birth to Jesus of Nazareth and the early Christian movement. I give thanks to my spiritual and theological teachers: John Akers, George (Shorty) Collins, John Cobb, David Ray Griffin, Bernard Loomer, Jack Verheyden, Richard Keady, and Ben White.

I have learned much about scripture from courses I've taught at congregations: First Christian Church, Tucson, Arizona; Palisades Community Church, Washington D.C.; and Falls Church Christian Church, Falls Church, Virginia. I give great thanks to South Congregational Church, United Church of Christ, whose generosity of spirit has allowed me to be not only pastor, teacher, and spiritual leader, but also a writer. The beauty of our Cape Cod village with its ponds, beaches, streams, and beaches has inspired my writing, preaching, and teaching. It is a daily joy to be part of a community that seeks to learn, love, and live the word of God.

I am grateful to Deborah Arca of Patheos (patheos.com), who encouraged me to write a weekly lectionary commentary for this forward-thinking spiritual website. As always, I give thanks for my companion of over 35 years, Kate, whose partnership in ministry, parenting, grand parenting, and family life has been at heart of my spiritual journey.

Finally, I give thanks for you and your quest for faithful excellence in preaching. May these words be an inspiration and creativity in responding to God's word and wisdom in your life.

Pentecost 2014

CHAPTER ONE
MARK'S HOLY ADVENTURE

Mark is on the move. The word "immediately" shows up throughout the text. Mark's Jesus is a pilgrim teacher and preacher, whose message is also on the move, expanding the theological, geographical, and ethnic boundaries of faith.

The spiritual landscape of Mark is stark and sometimes threatening. We travel down dusty roads, senses keen to detect bandits. We step aside for Roman occupation troops, knowing that the hint of insubordination could lead to imprisonment. We face storms at sea and waves threaten to capsize our boats. Religious leaders plot Jesus' death and a cross awaits the healer.

Jesus is always on the move with crowds following him, looking for a meaningful word that will heal their souls or energetic touch that will transform their cells. Jesus speaks for God, finding his authority in God's affirmation, "you are my beloved son." Jesus teaches and preaches God's good news and the good news he reveals is holistic and concrete. Jesus' words cast out demons and welcome sinners. His table is for all and in this table fellowship a new kind of family is born, composed of the most unlikely hodgepodge of companions: tax collectors and fishermen, women and persons recovering from the trauma and mental illness, Gentiles and Jews.

Jesus' vision of God's realm is on the move, too. Luke tells us that Jesus grew in wisdom and stature. (Luke 2:52) Mark gives us a picture of Jesus' growth process through times of prayerful solitude and encounters with persons of other ethnicities. Mark's Jesus speaks for God in the here and now as a real person, and not a Johannine pre-existent metaphysical figure. Mark has no room for the intricacies of creedal Christianity. His Jesus is fully alive and fully in touch with God. There is no confusion between the divine and human in Jesus; no dualism of the "human part" and the "divine part" of our Savior. He is one person with one great desire, to bring God's realm into everyday life and to challenge whatever diminishes the embodiment of God's vision in human life. The living, flesh and blood Jesus unites body, mind, and spirit in full attunement with God's vision for his life. Heaven is real, but heaven can wait. Now is the day to share God's good news, heal the sick, awaken dull spirits, and invite the world to come alive.

Even when Jesus gets cranky as he appears to have been in dialogue with the Syrophoenician woman, facing off with the religious leaders, or when he is threatened by the crowds, his ill humor is also a reflection of his whole person relationship with God. His whole emotional life is directed toward God. Jesus reflects what Jewish theologian Abraham Joshua Heschel describes as the "divine pathos," a complete joining of the divine and human passions for justice and healing. Small details matter to the author of Mark's Gospel, just as they did to the Hebraic prophets, and they matter to Jesus as well. His concern embraced a woman with a fever which prevented her from supervising dinner arrangements; the need for a child recently aroused from a coma to have a good meal; and failure of his disciples to have time to eat or refresh their spirits.

Mark's Jesus is one of us, fully human in all of its dimensions. He is also what we might become if we let go of our egos and attuned our wills with God's vision. This earliest gospel writer truly knew the continuity of divine and human in Jesus. His words prefigured the insights of the author of the last of the canonical gospels, who describes Jesus as affirming that we can do greater things than him. (John 14:12) You can imagine, sometimes with fear and trembling, sharing a meal with Jesus, accompanying him on a journey through the wilderness or sailing on the Galilean lake. Mark's Jesus enjoys a good meal and the laughter of celebrations and is willing to bend the rules to refresh his disciples or welcome an outcast.

Mark's Jesus grew to become comfortable with pluralism, first, with the diversity of the human condition challenging the temptation to divide humankind into insiders and outsiders, and then with ethnic and religious diversity. Mark's Jesus expands the circle of God's love to include the morally suspect and persons of other religious perspectives. He becomes our model for expanding the circle of grace to include humankind in all its wondrous diversity.

Mark's Jesus is a healer. More than any other gospel, Mark sees Jesus as the opponent of everything that limits human possibility whether the limitations are physical, spiritual, emotional, or relational.[1] Mark's Jesus invites us to take seriously today's growing evidence that prayer can be a factor in human well-being; religious commitment promotes good heath; and healing touch can transform cells and souls alike. I believe that Jesus would have been comfortable with our current integration of high tech and high touch. He would have recognized the value of other healers, including complementary medical care givers such as reiki practitioners, acupuncturists, qigong teachers, and yoga instructors as well as liturgical healers within our congregations.

Mark's Jesus is truly a suffering servant. He calls us beyond the individual ego to identify ourselves with the well-being of the whole earth. He takes on the suffering of the world, compassionately, devoting himself to the healing of the sick and challenging anyone who would stand in the way of God's healing touch. He calls us to die to the limited self-preoccupied and cramped ego to open to the spacious energy of God's vision. In taking up our cross, we die to the ruggedly individual self and discover the resurrection of God's self in ourselves, blessing us beyond anything for which we can ask or imagine.

Reading Mark will inspire your own journeys as pastors, teachers, and preachers. Let Mark's Jesus awaken you to the glory of God, residing in your life and within your congregation. Let the adventures begin with Jesus as your companion!

---

[1] For more on Mark's healing vision see Bruce Epperly, *Healing Marks: Healing and Spirituality in Mark's Gospel* (Gonzales, FL, 2012).

CHAPTER TWO
PREACHING AND THE SPIRIT

Preaching is a spiritual task. It is the most sustained form of spiritual and intellectual formation for most pastors. For nearly fifty weeks each year, preachers pore over the lectionary readings, seeking insights to share with their congregants. The preaching task, at its best, encompasses and connects mind, body, and spirit, relationships in the congregation, and dialogue with world events. Preaching is a dialogue taking place on holy ground. When I prepare my sermons, I visualize my congregation at South Congregational Church, ponder the highways and byways and beaches and ponds of Cape Cod, and consider the latest news in the *Cape Cod Times*, *Barnstable Patriot*, and on television and radio news. I ponder the daily lives of the people I will see on Sunday morning. I also take my sermons on a prayer walk, winding my way on the three mile roundtrip from my church study on Main Street in the village of Centerville to the Craigville Retreat Center. On the way I discover new insights and ways to look at the text, and discover new possibilities for sharing good news with my congregation. Sometimes ideas soar like the osprey on Covell's Beach, other times they glide smoothly like the swans on Lake Elizabeth. Still other times they swirl chaotically like the sands of Craigville and Long beaches.

I see preaching as an adventure of the spirit. Preaching provides provocative possibilities and new images for preacher and congregants alike. Our most inspirational sermons begin where we are and take us toward new horizons of faithful adventure in companionship with an adventurous God. Accordingly, I have divided each week's lectionary adventure in two parts. The first section is composed of a homiletical commentary, divided in three parts: a commentary on the text, practical applications of the text ("So What?"), and roads not travelled (wild ideas that you just might preach if you had no fear about losing your job!). My approach is theological and experiential; I leave biblical exegesis to other commentators. This approach reflects my own belief that the

12

scriptures of the day are intended to be the beginning not the end of the preacher's task. Our sermons are best when they move from the approach of "back to the bible" to "forward from God's word and wisdom." Scripture always takes us beyond the words to the living Wisdom of a pilgrim and personal God. The second section is composed of spiritual practices for preachers and families at church: spiritual affirmations, a spiritual practice for preachers, and practices whose purpose is to edify and expand on the scriptural passage throughout the week.

My ultimate goal is not only to provide homiletical guidance and inspiration but to deepen your spiritual life and enable the process of preaching itself, as well as your sermon preparation, to be integral to your spiritual growth. I believe that week after week and in season and out, we can – like Jesus and his followers – go to a deserted place, refresh our spirits, and return with compassion for our congregants and inspiration to share God's good news, always new every morning, that will bring insight, healing, and challenge to our congregations and seekers. Our study can be prayer, and our prayers can transform our congregations and the world.

A Word about Perspective. This text emerges from the reflections of a working preacher. I have preached regularly for nearly thirty five years, and recall having preached my first sermon as a college student in 1973. My preaching has evolved in my integration of the study, classroom, and pulpit. Insights have abounded that have shaped my ministry, inspired by the realities of pastoral ministry – hospital rooms and hospices, maternity wards and gravesides, playing with children and listening to elders, responding to crises of faith and baptizing new believers. My theology has shaped my preaching and my preaching has transformed my theology. My theological orientation is process-relational: I believe God is intimate, interactive, and dynamic. What we do matters to God, and God is constantly at work in all things. Process theology is often identified with the liberal and progressive movements in Christianity. My progressive and liberal perspectives are not merely intellectual; they are shaped by the tradition of Christian mysticism, the lively healing ministry of Jesus and today's healing and holistic health and complementary medicine movements, evangelical experience, ecumenism, and the encounter with other religious traditions.

13

South Congregational Church, United Church of Christ, in Centerville, Massachusetts, speaks of being a village church with a global perspective, and this would be a good description of my own approach, profoundly local and personal, but also concerned with global and international issues. My preaching vision blends concern with threats to butterflies, whales, and the delicate Cape Cod ecosystem, and the proliferation of substance abuse on the Cape, and also the realities of global climate change, world hunger, sexual trafficking, and violence among nations. In the spirit of John Wesley, I believe my parish is the world and that we bring well-being to the global by our concern for the local. I also believe, with Puritan preacher John Robinson, that more light can be shed on the scriptures. Being a preacher is an adventure of spiritual imagination. Let Mark lead the way, and let the adventures begin!

THE SEASON OF ADVENT: STARK EXPECTATION

Mark cuts to the chase. There are no magi or shepherds in Mark. Absent is the angelic chorus, the annunciation to Mary, the virgin birth, and Joseph's dream. Mark begins with the adult Jesus, prepared to be baptized and then ready to go public to preach the good news of God's coming realm.

There are no "lost years of Jesus" in Mark. Nor is there the description of Jesus as the word made flesh, the incarnation of God's world-creating wisdom. All important for Mark is Jesus' public ministry: salvation is a matter of action, divine and human, in this world of mortality, sin, and death. If we follow God's way today, metaphysical speculation will take care of itself and our future adventures will be joyful!

The emergence of Jesus as a public teacher and healer opens the world to new and unexpected possibilities. Jesus' ministry raises expectations for the way the world can become. The season of Advent still raises expectations for us and challenges us to close the gap between what is and what can be. Without fanfare, Mark invites us to experience God's good news amid the threats, ambiguity, and challenges of our own lives. Even if Mark does not treat us to a Christmas story, he gives us hope that we can be born anew and that the child who grew up to be savior can be born in us.

First Sunday in Advent
Mark 13:24-37

Advent joins *chronos* and *kairos*, evenly-moving clock time and unique, transformative moments that change everything. Today's reading reflects on the goal of clock time, yet is filled with meaning in the present moment, this very moment. We are to live as if in each moment Christ comes to us in ways that will bring joy and growth to our world. Christ's glorious coming can be experienced now, and need not be deferred to some apocalyptic catastrophe-escape.

For over two thousand years, Christians have attempted to discern the signs of the times. Believing history is moving toward its dramatic culmination, some have sold their property, and headed to the mountains to secure the best seats to view Christ's return and be among the first to be lifted up to the heavens. Others have made millions writing books about the Second Coming, identifying it with a collision with an asteroid, the four red moons, conflict in the Middle East, and tension with the Soviet Union. Even the presidency of Ronald Wilson Reagan was cited as a precursor to the final battle between Christ and Satan. After all, the letters of his name add up to "6-6-6!" One thing all these end time speculations have had in common is that they have always been wrong and required readjustments and further readjustments in light of new interpretations of biblical prophesies. Further, virtually all of them turn our attention from our role in responding to political and social problems in favor of anticipating a divine rescue operation that will solve our problems and create a new world system without any efforts, other than doctrinal orthodoxy, on our part. If we are among the chosen or have uttered the right words, the world can go to hell and we'll be alright, for God will lift us up beyond life's tragedies and give us a front row seat to earth's destruction.

Perhaps, there should be a moratorium on end time speculation. Apocalyptic prophecies provide virtually no spiritual benefit for struggling humanity, encourage passivity in issues of social justice and earth care, and inspire a curious negativity in which adherents believe "the bad news is the good news." Many end-time and conservative Christians challenge the evidence of global climate change because it suggests humans and not God will usher in the destruction of human and non-human life. Such approaches to the future lead many to stereotype Christians as so heavenly minded that they are no earthly good. Moreover, despite their apparent piety, these end-time believers act as if they can use the earth's resources as they choose without regard to the well-being of the environment, since God will soon destroy the earth with fire and brimstone. At a time in which, we need to be more socially and environmentally responsible, they lure us away from the world whose value God so cherished that, as John 3:16 asserts, God sent the Christ the only Son

16

to save. Jettisoning apocalyptic speculation might guide us toward another type of eschatological living, a full human life grounded in the recognition that this unrepeatable moment, right now, is the *kairos*, the right time, indeed, God's time for us to say "yes" and become new creations.

Mark believes that there will be hard times in the future, and we can see them on the horizon as well. Mark sees continuity between human and cosmic history. We are connected with the seasons and the planets. Their movements shape our destinies and reflect God's deeper wisdom, Mark believes, and as we have discovered in the past fifty years, our actions, reflected in the impact of technology and consumerism on the environment, are reshaping the seasons meteorologically. Just as Jesus' spiritual power was able to still the storms on the Sea of Galilee, we have the ability to influence the weather around us mostly for the worse as a result of the impact of our own spiritual and economic values.

Mark, then, turns to the lesson of the fig tree, whose cycle of growth alerts us to the seasons of the year. We need to be aware of the seasons of God's presence in the world. God's presence in history is not homogenous, but variable and intimate. God's vision changes in the call and response of history and with changes in God's vision come new possibilities and challenges for those who are attentive.

God is faithful through all the seasons of life and changes in the social and natural orders. God's word will not pass away and the living God's mercies are new every morning. The passage concludes with a call to spiritual awareness and mindful discipleship. No one knows the time of God's coming. We need to stay awake, observing the signs of the times, and responding according to God's moment-by-moment call. "Keep awake!" Jesus urges.

Faithful wakefulness involves pausing and noticing what's going on around us in our families, neighborhoods, communities, nation, and the planet. We are often so busy that we fail to see the budding fig tree or the blossoming cherry tree even though it is right in front of us. We are too hurried to see the child in need of our attention, the homeless person in need of a meal, and family members going through difficult times. But, as Jesus says, your response to them is also a response to me. God knows because God feels – God is touched by our joys and sorrows, and our responses to crises around us.

Keep awake! The coming of Christ is moment by moment, not once and for all. Pray with your eyes open, discerning the presence of God in your daily encounters, in friends and family members, and passersby. Leo Tolstoy tells the story of a village shoemaker, Martin, who has a dream in which he hears Jesus tell him that he will visit him the next day.[2] Martin wakes up with excitement, expecting the coming of Christ in the course of his workday. From his window, Martin can observe the feet of everyone who passes by. He recognizes the passersby by their footwear, having crafted or repaired most of the villagers' shoes. As the morning passes, he sees an old man shoveling snow and invites him in for a cup of hot tea. Later that day, he observes a poorly dressed woman carrying her baby. Her clothing is insufficient to warm her or her baby. He invites her in for a meal and gives her his late wife's coat. As the day progresses, he observes a scuffle outside and rushes out to intervene on behalf of a starving boy, who has been apprehended for stealing an apple from an elderly vendor. He makes peace between the two, and purchases an apple for the boy.

As day ends and he eats his evening meal, Martin recollects his day and wonders why Jesus did not keep his promise. To his surprise, Christ comes to him, showing him the faces of the old soldier, the young girl and her baby, and the boy, and reminding him, "As you have unto to the least of these, my brothers and sisters, you have done unto me." As Paul, was to say to Jesus' followers in Rome, "now is the accepted time, now is the day of salvation." God is here, God is now, and God is with you. That is Mark's Advent message.

So What? The season of Advent invites the pastor and his or her community to stay awake. The flurry of Christmas activities can dull our senses and plunge us into oblivious busyness, when we need to be most mindful of God's presence in our daily encounters. Prayerful wakefulness reminds us of the often unnoticed growth in ourselves and our congregations, and opens us to God's coming in

---

[2] Leo Tolstoy, "Where Love Is, God Is." See http://www.online-literature.com/tolstoy/2892/

each moment and encounter of life. Martin Luther is reputed to have said, "I have so much to do, I need to spend more time in prayer." The busyness of Advent and the days leading up to Christmas are a call to put our spiritual practices of prayer and meditation at the heart of our daily adventures.

Preparing for Christ's return in this very moment means that we commit ourselves to becoming aware of our spiritual state. Are we so caught up in the culture of consumption that we miss Christ's birthing in our lives? What aspects of the Christmas season do we need to prune away to midwife the coming of Christ in our lives and the world?

Roads Not Travelled. As you read the passage from Mark, let your mind wander toward far off and unexpected places. What wild and crazy ideas bubble up? The roads not taken in our homiletic adventures – the ones that are just too off the beaten path or unsettling to us and our congregation – shape our sermons even if we never share them with others.

As I pondered this passage, I thought of putting posters up in the sanctuary with the faces of popular evangelists and teachers and quotes detailing their prognostications about the Second Coming, and then under each in bright red letters, write "proved wrong" or "wrong again." I also thought of a saying attributed to Martin Luther: If I were told that the world would end tomorrow, I'd plant a tree. This inspired me to have a shout out about what tree congregants would plant, and place posters up with two options: pictures of destruction and pictures of beauty, with the question beneath them, "Which is God's way of dealing with our planet?"

SPIRITUAL PRACTICES
FOR THE PREACHER AND CONGREGATION

Affirmative Faith. This week's passages invite the pastor and congregation to stay awake in challenging times. Repeating the following affirmations, or an affirmation of your choice throughout the week will enable you to more fully discern God's presence in the busyness of the Advent season at church and home.

I am awake to God's presence throughout the day.
Christ is coming to me right now, I will greet him with love.

A Spiritual Practice for the Preacher. Spiritual guide Gerald May invited his readers to pause, notice, open, yield and stretch, and then respond to God's presence in the events of their lives.[3] In this practice, simply pause throughout the day, perhaps between appointments, as you log onto to your computer or check messages, or enter the church building. Take a moment to look around and observe your inner life as well as the environment around you. Prayerfully open to any insights that emerge in your momentary pauses with the willingness to yield and respond to a deeper wisdom than your own.

Faith at Home. Throughout the week, invite members of your family to take moments for stillness. Young children can pause to sit beside you or in a favorite chair to take a few breaths. Certain moments can call you to prayerful awareness: stopping at a red light, checking your Facebook or Twitter account, sitting down for a meal, and saying "good bye" to a child or spouse going to school or work. Moments dedicated to stillness transform time: we still live in the world of clock time and our daily activities, but time can become more abundant, spacious, and full. In regularly pausing, we discover that we have enough time to do our daily tasks. We may also become more attentive to the seasons of our life and prioritize our tasks more creatively and insightfully, discovering the difference between the necessary and optional activities of life. We may learn to do less and enjoy more; and become faithfully excellent in our daily responsibilities as a result of our awareness of God's vision for this holy here and holy now.

Second Sunday of Advent
Mark 1:1-8

The beginning of the gospel of Jesus Christ: Mark introduces some of the most enduring words in human history in the most minimalist fashion. Like the iconic character, Joe Friday, from the television series "Dragnet," Mark is initially interested in

---

[3] Gerald May, *The Awakened Heart* (New York: Harper, 1993).

just the facts, events that can be verified and demonstrated for the whole world to see. There are no magi and shepherds, and no angelic choruses and messages from the heavens. The angelic visitation to young Mary is of no importance to the author of the first gospel. There is no mention of Joseph's revelatory dream, or a virgin birth. Mark is interested in the message, the good news of God's coming realm embodied and revealed in the life and teachings of Jesus, God's all so human and earthy beloved one. Mark's Jesus truly embodies the last canonical gospel's affirmation that Jesus is God's word and wisdom made flesh and embodied in the messiness of history. (John 1:1-14)

Revelation and incarnation are always historical and contextual. Jesus' message builds on the prophetic tradition and its first century embodiment in John the Baptist. God's grace and truth require preparation and John prepares the way for God's messenger to humankind. Revelation, for Mark, may be dropped from the sky – the descent of the Spirit at Jesus' baptism – but it also emerges from below, from the to and fro of daily life and personal encounters.

Rough and tumble John has a simple and direct message. "Repent, turn your life around, and be baptized." Transformation requires reformation and the injection of something new into our personal and community histories. Baptism signifies our willingness to become companions on God's adventure of personal and social renewal. Old ways and behaviors that prevent us from living into God's coming realm must be jettisoned. Half-heartedness will not do. We need to plunge into God's realm literally and figuratively.

In Mark's portrait of John the Baptist, John's selflessness stands out. He has let go of any possessiveness or need to be at the center of attention. He is clear that his vocation is call humankind to transformation and that the fullness of transformation will come through the coming Jesus. At the right time, the *kairos* moment, John will exit making room for God's coming savior and teacher.

Mark is not prone to speculation. He is concerned, even when he speaks of Jesus' miraculous power to heal mind, body, and spirit, and to effect changes in the non-human world of storm and wind, with what can be publically observed or spiritually experienced. Still, we can take some speculative liberties regarding the relationship of John and Jesus. God's initiative is at the heart of both boys' births. When Mary becomes unexpectedly pregnant, she leaves her hometown to stay with Elizabeth, John's mother. Fetal John jumps for joy in welcome of Jesus' mother. I suspect that John and Jesus were close friends, played together, studied together, and perhaps left home to study with the Essene community. I believe that they were spiritual friends, *anamcara*, who shared each other's journeys and mirrored each other's vocational destinies. I imagine that when Jesus came to John to be baptized, John affirmed Jesus' unique vocation as he welcomed him as friend and brother, and not a stranger. For John, being second fiddle felt like first string as he fulfilled his vocation to clear the underbrush for Jesus' public ministry.

So What? Today's reading invites us to our own personal and community repentance. This begins with self-examination and mindfulness. We need to ask ourselves: What stands in the way of our commitment to God's realm in our personal, professional, and community life? Where is our congregation entrapped by our culture's death-filled values? Where do we need a change of heart and change of focus as a community? If we want to be ready for Christ in our midst, we have a lot of spiritual pruning to do.

Roads Not Travelled. The preacher can enlist a layperson to suddenly enter the worship space, dressed in a cloak and shouting, "Repent, repent and turn form sin to salvation" or some variation. Wildly gesturing, your "John" can challenge congregants to come forward to be sprinkled with water on their hands or foreheads as a sign of their repentance.

SPIRITUAL PRACTICES
FOR THE PREACHER AND CONGREGATION

Affirmative Faith. Throughout the week, recite the following affirmations to keep you in touch with God's vision for your life and community.

> *I let go of everything that stands in the way of my embodiment of God's vision.*
> *I prepare the way for Jesus' coming in every encounter.*
> *I turn toward God's new life for myself and others.*

A Spiritual Practice for Preachers. John the Baptist's message calls preachers and congregants to self-examination and mindfulness. As Paul was to say to an early Christian community, "be not conformed to this world, but be transformed by the renewing of your mind." (Romans 12:2) In the personal and pastoral-liturgical busyness of the Advent-Christmas season, take time to prayerfully ask yourself the following questions:

- Where am I conforming to cultural rather than Christ-like values in my personal life and pastoral leadership?
- What is my current state of spiritual well-being? Am I open to Christ's presence or am I caught up in the frenetic pace of the season?
- Am I taking time for prayer and meditation? Or, is the busyness of Christmas preparations standing in the way of my finding a quiet center in the course of each day's activities?

Along with self-examination, make a commitment to take twenty minutes each day for times for prayer, meditation, and devotional reading, over and above your sermon and worship preparation. When you begin to feel busy, make a choice to pause and open to God's presence quietly being born in your life. Prayer and meditation transform our experience of time, giving us a sense of greater spaciousness and prioritizing the commitments of our lives.

Faith at Home. At least once this week, take time for a family conversation on what's truly important at Christmastime. You may do this as part of a family prayer and worship time, according to the following pattern or a pattern of your choice:

- Light a candle, accompanied by a prayer such as, "Enlighten us with your wisdom, O God. Let your light shine in us, so that our love burns bright."
- Reflect on those things and persons for which you are most thankful.

23

- Take a few moments for stillness. (Even young children can be still for a moment.)
- Read a scripture such as Matthew 5:13-16. (You are the light of the world; you are the salt of the earth.) Share what it means.

Share around the family table one way you can experience God's light and the deepest meaning of Christmas.

Close with a blessing for each family member, praying for each and asking God to help you be lights in the world.

THE SEASON OF EPIPHANY
DISCOVERING GOD ON THE PATHWAY

Epiphany is the season of revealing. What has been hidden becomes visible. God's grace becomes embodied in daily life. The earthly Jesus is seen as infinite, light-filled, and life-transforming. The Celtic Christian tradition uses the term "thin place" to describe the intersection of heaven and earth, infinite and finite, and eternal and temporal. All places are potential thin places in our God-filled world. Still, we are often oblivious to God's revelations until, like Jacob awakening from his dream of a ladder of angels, we proclaim in astonishment, "God was in this place and I did not know it."

At his baptism, Jesus receives God's blessing and affirmation as "God's beloved child." God's Spirit descends on him, filling him with insight and energy. Jesus claims his role as messenger and embodiment of God's realm. He shares good news, and he also *is* good news to those whom he meets. He reveals God's presence as a fully alive human, mediating the light of God from which the universe emerged.

Mark's epiphanies help us experience our own epiphanies and thin places in the midst of the ordinary and challenging events of life. In flesh and blood, God comes alive and gives the energy of new life to change the world.

The Baptism of Jesus
Mark 1:4-11

"You are my beloved child in whom I am well-pleased." So says God to Jesus as he is being baptized by John. "You are my beloved child in whom I am well-pleased." So says God to each one of us as we are baptized.

Baptism is a ritual of God's grace. It is more than water, and more than ritual. We are God's beloved, whether or not we are

25

baptized. Baptism tells each of us that, even if we don't remember it, we are loved beyond measure and we don't have to earn or do anything about it.

Many Christians make baptism a "work" or an example of what Martin Luther described as "works righteousness." They believe that we have to be baptized at a certain age, by a certain method, and by certain authorized people for it to be efficacious. They even make salvation dependent on whether or not we've been baptized. God's Spirit works within our rituals, but does not depend upon our rituals, even those instituted by Jesus and the early church. If baptism becomes a "work," operative only according to certain principles, it becomes an instrument of fear and control, and not an act of liberation and love.

I relish being a grandparent. It is the fruition of good parenting and the love I have for my son and his wife. When my daughter-in-law was expecting, I came to love each of these little boys. Long before they were born, they were the apples of my eye. When they were born and all they could do was sleep, cry, pee, and poop, I loved them. Before they could do anything, I loved them. I believe that God is at least as loving toward creation as I am toward my grandchildren, whom I baptized as infants.

Baptism means this: I love you, you are mine, and nothing you can do can disqualify you from my love. As John Ylvisaker's hymn says, I was there to hear your cry at birth and followed you through your journey, from birth to death, rejoicing in baptism and welcoming you home with one more surprise, God's eternal life.[4]

Martin Luther often suffered from severe depression. During the worst times of depression, when he gave up on everything else and doubted his faith and ministry, he scribbled on his desk, "I was baptized." That meant all the difference in the world to him: God's promise, revealed in baptism is certain, non-negotiable, and never ending. It's not about us or our goodness, but about a divine love as great as the love we have for our spouses, children, grandchildren, and best friends.

Today, we remember that grace is visible in the acts of worship and daily life. Grace is alive in our churches and ministries and in the welcome of each newborn child. Let's celebrate God's

---

[4] John Ylvisaker, "I Was There to Hear Your Borning Cry."

love and our kinship with God's beloved child, whose love encompasses, welcomes, and heals all of us.

So What? Baptism can change everything. While not necessary for salvation, it is a tangible promise, like a wedding ring, of vows made; in this case, the vows of a faith community and God's vows to us. Remembering our baptisms challenges us to trust God in all the seasons of life and to share our faith with others in tangible acts of love.

Roads Not Travelled. Baptism needs to be acted out in daily life and worship. The preacher can process as service begins sprinkling holy water on everyone in church as a reminder and an opportunity to renew our baptisms.

In considering the nature of baptism, the preacher can consider whether or not baptism is necessary to salvation. If it isn't, then he or she can ask, "Why are we baptized? What difference does it make?" and invite the congregation to be part of a theological dialogue on baptism and the scope of salvation. How do we live out our baptism in inclusive ways on a day to day basis?

SPIRITUAL PRACTICES
FOR THE PREACHER AND THE CONGREGATION

Affirmative Faith. In the spirit of Jesus' baptism, let us affirm that we are God's beloved children, whether or not we have been baptized.

> *I am baptized in God's love.*
> *Each morning I am refreshed by God's living waters.*
> *God renews and transforms me every day, liberating me from*
> *the past and opening me to this holy moment.*

A Spiritual Practice for Preachers. This week, remember your baptism. Most of us take a daily shower. Your daily shower can become a religious ritual. Each day, when you shower or bathe, visualize the waters flowing over your body, cleansing and refreshing you. As you shower, let go of any burdens or stress. Experience your shower as God's blessing and cleansing so that you can begin again, aware of your identity as God's beloved child.

Faith at Home. When Jesus came out of the waters of baptism, he heard God's voice proclaiming "you are my beloved child." I am sure that he was transformed by these words and the spiritual energy that went with them. Baptism is God's pronouncement on each of us as beloved. Throughout the week, see and treat the members of your family as God's beloved children. This does not mean letting bad behavior or impoliteness go unnoticed; it does mean that we address each other with love, respect, and affirmation, regardless of the circumstances of family life. In the spirit of the Benedictine monastic tradition, treat everyone as Christ, as holy and as reflecting God's loving creativity.

You might also consider inviting members of your family to see their baths and showers as a way of beginning again, and embracing God's mercies, always new and inspiring with each new morning.

Third Sunday after the Epiphany
Mark 1:14-20

There is always a right time for transformation and revelation. This is the *kairos* moment when everything falls into place and we embrace God's call to wholeness. After the arrest of John the Baptist, it's Jesus' right time to go public and share his vision of God's message to humankind. Although Jesus' message involves turning from one pathway to another, the heart of Jesus' vision is good news. The realm of God is good news for everyone who responds to Jesus' call, and everyone is invited.

As followers of Jesus, we need to explore the nature of his good news and how we are to embody it in our time. Good news is not static, but constantly changing in form and media. Jesus' good news involved hospitality to outcasts, affirmation of women and children, healing of the sick, defeating the demonic, and calling people to live out these same values in their everyday lives. Jesus' message was shaped by his social and political context as a member of an occupied people with little or no political power. Jesus' realm did not challenge directly the political authority of the Roman

28

Empire, although Jesus message was – and is now - implicitly subversive of any political, economic, relational, or religious hierarchy and domination system.

What is our good news? This question is addressed to congregations in their local setting and also their global context. We may have our own nuance to Jesus' message, appropriate to your congregational and community setting, but surely it must involve healing, hospitality, spiritual renewal, and sacrifice. It must be a message of mission to the poor, marginalized, and vulnerable, and this message is political even if we don't share it in terms of the win-lose approach of today's political system. If anything, we may be the most countercultural, when we embody a politics of compassion and reconciliation; choosing love and life in the "what" and "how" of our message.

Our good news is also global. Where I pastor on Cape Cod, Massachusetts, our good news must include the saving the good earth, nurturing the growth of Monarch Butterflies, protecting the ponds, lakes, and oceans, providing backpacks and school supplies for neighborhood children, a place for twelve step groups, and food for the hungry. Our mission leads far beyond the Cape to embrace care for global climate change, and its impact on our delicate ecosystem, planetary weather patterns, and seacoast areas across the globe.

Jesus' good news catches the imagination of a cohort of working fishermen. Taken literally, the story of the call of Peter, Andrew, James, and John suggests that they followed immediately without any prior relationship to Jesus. In contrast, I believe that an imaginative reading of this passage might paint the following picture of the call of the first disciples. I believe Jesus got to know the fishermen before asking for a personal decision on their part. They might have shared stories of their professions, ate meals together, talked about God's realm, and fished together. Peter, James, John, and Andrew might have spent time in conversation with their wives, prepared financially for their well-being, and insured that there would be sufficient relational support. Perhaps, over the course of their ministry, these disciples returned home regularly to be with their spouses and nurture their children. Still, these men – and others, both women and men – followed Jesus, sacrificing comfort to be part of Jesus' coming realm.

29

To some, my imaginative approach might seem too half-hearted and prudent. In response, however, I believe that although our following Jesus may mean a radical break from life as usual, and from hearth and home, for most people, the process of committing ourselves to Christ involves a gradual transformation of values and a turning from self-absorption to care for others and from self-interest to spiritual stature in which the needs of others are as important as one's own. However we move forward God's realm, it is good news!

So What? Is it possible to connect prudence with discipleship? Or, care with risk-taking? Or sacrifice while insuring the well-being of your family? If, as the Jewish tradition asserts, the world is saved whenever one soul finds wholeness, the care of Peter's – and the others' – families is important, too. Too many ministers have neglected their own children to take care of other peoples' children and unintentionally created feelings of alienation from church, family, and God among their family members. Other ministers have neglected their spouses to insure the well-being of other peoples' marriages and have suffered the consequences of their neglect.

Good news embraces our lives in their entirety. We must act locally – honoring our families and communities – while thinking globally beyond our family and community concerns.

In that way, healing can encompass the whole earth and our own neighborhoods one person at a time.

Roads Not Travelled. God's good news involves sacrifice. Too often we get by – and I am speaking as a pastor to pastors – through what Dietrich Bonhoeffer called "cheap grace." We are too prudent. As an act of spiritual pulse taking, the pastor can confess his sin of prudence and share his or her struggles to do something big for God. The pastor can make an altar call, inviting people to come forward to make a big commitment to God.

The pastor might also ask people to prepare for this passage by a provocative question such as "What's your good news?" or "If you had only one thing to say about your faith, what would it be?"

SPIRITUAL PRACTICES
FOR THE PREACHER AND CONGREGATION

Affirmative Faith. We are called to embody Christ's good news one moment and person at a time. Affirmations keep us in touch with God's vision in all the details of life.

I share God's good news in every encounter.
I am faithful to my family and loved ones as well as to strangers.
I answer God's call to wholeness and love throughout the day.

A Spiritual Practice for Preachers. In this practice, take some time to be still in God's presence, opening to God by breathing calmly and gently. After a few minutes, begin to visualize your loved ones. Experience them being filled and surrounded by God's light. See them as Christ sees them. As calm descends, ask God to give you guidance about how you can most deeply care for your family while being faithful to sharing God's good news in your ministry.

Faith at Home. Home life is the crucible for spiritual transformation. We are often most impatient and insulting to those under our own roofs. Jesus' good news reminds us to be good news givers in our families. In the spirit of last week's commentary, consider what good news you can share in your home. What words of kindness can you say? How can you embody a spirit of self-sacrifice in your family? If you are a parent, how can you balance the responsibilities entailed in your professional career with care for your family obligations? How can you reach out to the community for Christ and give the same attention to your family?

Fourth Sunday after the Epiphany
Mark 1:21-28

This past summer, I preached a series entitled "The Questions Kids Ask," based on themes suggested by the children and youth of our church. One of topics that emerged was "What is the Devil?" The Fourth Sunday after the Epiphany introduces a theme that is present throughout Mark's gospel – Jesus' sovereignty over evil or unclean spirits. God's realm is intended to bring beauty and health to all creation, and challenges everything that stands in the way of human well-being.

Despite our modern skepticism about the supernatural and spiritual world, stories about spirit possession, exorcism, zombies, and ghosts abound in the media and popular literature. While such stories are often fabricated, they reveal our interest in realities beyond the technologically-controlled and apparently safe world described by modern rationalists. We have an inkling that there may be realities beneath or beyond everyday consciousness that can take possession of people like ourselves. We have a suspicion that some places, institutions, and persons may be controlled by spirits, who have the intention to harm us and those we love. We have first-hand experience of mental illness, substance abuse, and the proliferation of addictive behaviors. Every so often, we may feel overpowered by spiritual and emotional energies that subvert the best interests of the rational mind.

In an intricately interdependent and evolving world, we cannot categorically deny subhuman or superhuman powers that can overwhelm the rational mind. The reality of unclean or evil spirits doesn't fit into the modern world view. Although we use psychological terms to describe what the ancients attributed to evil spirits, this change in terminology in no way minimizes the pain people feel when they experience themselves as attacked by powers beyond themselves.

Today, only a handful of spiritual leaders perform exorcisms or affirm the existence of evil spirits. Based on this reality, many pastors might be tempted to eliminate this passage altogether. Still, it deserves some consideration since Jesus' conflict with evil spirits is an essential aspect of Mark's good news. Jesus' victory over the demonic is a sign of his intimacy with God. Jesus has authority over all creation, human and non-human, and spiritual and physical. God's realm redeems and transforms every aspect of life, liberating all captives, whether their captivity is physical, emotional, political, or psychological.

In the first century, illness was attributed to many factors, including God's will, divine punishment for sin, and evil spirits. The impact of evil spirits reflected a type of spiritual germ theory, in which illness of body, mind, and spirit was caused by external forces, completely beyond the control of the victim. The malevolent spirit might render its occupant unclean, but her or his outcast status was arbitrary and not the result of behavior, lifestyle, social standing, or livelihood. The cost was great, both personally and socially. One not only lost one's mind, one also lost any meaningful place in the social order and became, not unlike many persons suffering from mental illness in our time, a nuisance, threat, or virtual non-person.

Regardless of our attitude toward the existence of evil spirits, most of us have experienced glimpses of the demonic in our lives. Accounts of spiritual malevolence that poisons relationships, persons, and institutions are found in texts such as George McLain's *Claiming All Things for God,* Scott Peck's *People of the Lie;* Lloyd Rediger's *Clergy Killers;* and Walter Wink's *Naming the Powers.* Whole countries, such as Hitler's Germany, can be possessed by spirits of violence and hate, and year after year, congregations can make the same tragic mistakes, leading to the termination or resignation of pastor after pastor. There is no way on our own to defeat these malevolent influences, whether their origin is environmental, psychic, emotional, physiological, or spiritual; internal or external. Our only hope is prayerful turning to God and the presence of a healing community. Still, we might take comfort in Martin Luther's words from "A Mighty Fortress is Our God": although Satan's power and craft are great, and filled with cruel hate, one little word shall defeat Satan, and it is the word of Jesus Christ, who will win the battle against all that assails us.

So what? The existence of demonic forces, however, we understand them, is not an invitation to passivity, but to a robust faith. We must claim "the moral equivalent of war" in response to the forces of destruction. They call for a robust and active spirituality, willing to face destructive forces without polarization. A consideration of demonic or malign influences suggests the following:

- Don't deny the demonic.
- Don't focus on the demonic.
- Don't take on the demonic alone.
- Remember God is stronger than the forces of evil.
- Call on Jesus to protect and guide you.

Roads Not Travelled. The preacher can project on a screen a variety of images of the Evil One (Satan, Lucifer, the Devil) in the course of the sermon. He or she can also have a dialogue sermon with the Devil, portrayed by a member of the staff or a layperson. He can play, with permission, clips from the *Exorcist* and other films on demon possession.

SPIRITUAL PRACTICES
FOR THE PREACHER AND CONGREGATION

Affirmative Faith. In considering the forces of evil in our world, we need to put on an armor of light through transforming our thoughts and actions. Affirmations such as the following support a robust spirituality:

> *Nothing can separate me from the love of God in Christ Jesus.*
> *I am safe in God's loving care.*
> *I surround myself in God's love in every difficult encounter.*

A Spiritual Practice for Preachers. The Celtic tradition counsels a prayer for pilgrims called the "caim" or "prayer of encircling." In this prayer, while standing still, you draw a circle around yourself with your index finger. In the course of your encircling, you recite a prayer of protection, reminding you that wherever you travel, you are in God's hands.

Prayers of protection include the Prayer of St. Patrick or Lorica:

> Christ with me,
> Christ before me
> Christ behind me,
> Christ beneath me,
> Christ above me,
> Christ on my left,
> Christ on my right….
> Christ in every eye that sees me,
> Christ in every ear that hears me.
> Other prayers can be built upon:
> Nothing can separate me from the love of God.

34

God is with me wherever I go.
God's love surrounds and encircles me, protecting
me from all evil.

Faith at Home. Fear dominates many of our decisions and interactions. In family life, the Celtic caim or encircling is an antidote to fear. It places us in God's presence, and reminds us that wherever we are, we are in God's hands. In this prayer, while standing still, you draw a circle around yourself with your index finger. In the course of your encircling, you recite a prayer of protection, reminding you that wherever you travel, you are in God's hands. You can pray your encircling with St. Patrick:

> Christ with me,
> Christ before me
> Christ behind me,
> Christ beneath me,
> Christ above me,
> Christ on my left,
> Christ on my right….
> Christ in every eye that sees me,
> Christ in every ear that hears me.

Fifth Sunday after the Epiphany
Mark 1:29-39

For the next several Sundays, the lectionary readings focus on Jesus' healing ministry. Despite the identification of Luke as the Physician, Mark's Gospel is the healing gospel. We have already encountered Jesus' exorcism of an evil spirit and considered what both the diagnosis and cure of spirit possession might mean in light of 21st century Western and global medicine. The spiritual aspects of health and illness have been the subject of many books as well as scientific studies. While the research is not conclusive, it invites us to think of prayer, healing touch, and congregational involvement as complements to a healthy diet, exercise, and appropriate medical care.

The healing of Peter's mother-in-law is the centerpiece of this Sunday's lectionary reading. On the one hand, this healing raises issues of vocation and social standing. On the other hand, it shows us that no healing is too small for Jesus' consideration. This is not a life and death healing, but it involves reclaiming one's vocation and living out one's gifts in a particular time and place.

Jesus proclaimed that I have come that they might have abundant life. (John 10:10) Divine abundance encompasses every sphere of life from cradle to grave. Abundance is as much about the so-called secular as well as the so-called spiritual realms of life. In fact, we cannot clearly distinguish between secular and spiritual as realms of divine care. If God is present everywhere and in all things, then all activities are essentially holy.

Peter's mother-in-law has a minor illness that threatens her ability to welcome the teacher to her home. In first century Jewish society, the mother-in-law served as the primary hostess. Her task was to create a hospitable environment for guests and manage the family's domestic life. Peter's wife may have prepared the meal, but his mother-in-law supervised any social functions. As Peter's spiritual teacher, Jesus was a truly important guest, who deserved the highest level of hospitality.

Have you ever become ill prior to an important life event? Can you remember how you felt? I suspect Peter's mother-in-law felt the same sense of disappointment, anxiety, and failure at not being able to welcome and serve the teacher. Serving was at the heart of her vocation. This is not a matter of patriarchy or sexism, but context. Our vocations are always contextual, and in her case serving Jesus would have been the greatest of honors. But, now she can't even get out of her bed.

Jesus comes to her, takes her hand, and cures her fever. We are not given either the diagnosis or the cure. All we know is that Jesus restored her to wholeness and renewed her vocation. She may simply have had a case of the flu, but anyone who has come down with the flu or food poisoning knows how debilitating these otherwise self-limiting illnesses can be. You aren't going to die, but you feel and look like death warmed over!

Healing is at the heart of Mark's understanding of Jesus. Jesus restores minds, bodies, and spirits. He returns the unclean to society, restoring them interpersonally and vocationally. When word leaks out regarding Jesus' power to heal, crowds gather in search of physical, emotional, and spiritual relief. We can imagine Jesus creating a healing circle and working into the evening, responding to the pleas of Peter's neighbors. Perhaps, he only gets a few hours rest. As morning dawns, Jesus needs time for his own spiritual rejuvenation. The process of healing others can sap the energies of persons called to healing ministry. There is so much pain and need, and we feel compelled to address the miseries of humankind. But, there is also a time for rest. Health and wholeness require a dynamic balance of activity and rest, and action and contemplation.

Jesus goes to a quiet place for prayer. Jesus' morning prayers raise the questions: Why did Jesus need to pray? Wasn't he God's beloved, totally united with the divine parent? If so, why was prayer so pivotal to Mark's account of Jesus' ministry? Remember that Mark portrays a powerful, God-inspired, and earthly Jesus. Mark's Jesus was fully human and fully alive, and his unity with the divine parent took shape in finite human flesh and blood. Perhaps, Jesus needed to replenish his spiritual energy. Or, he may have needed to reconnect with God's vision for his life to obtain clarity and wisdom for the next steps of his ministry. Holistic and active spirituality must seek constant replenishment. We must, as Suzanne Schmidt asserts, run on plenty rather than empty in our personal and professional lives. In the spirit of Chinese medicine, which bears many affinities with Jesus' healing ministry, we need to be open to the healing energy flowing in and through us to others, and this often happens best through times of quiet receptivity and attunement with divine inspiration and energy.

So what? Often the church is a place of action rather than reflection. In liberal and progressive congregations, many members see the prophetic social activist approach as the heart of Christian faith. Problems are pressing and we can't take time for prayer and meditation; we need to respond immediately to global climate change, racism, sexism, and homophobia. Children need to be fed and persons need homes and health care, now! Taking time off for prayer and meditation seems a luxury when people are crying out for food and shelter. Jesus was aware of the depth of pain and our need for healing. Still, he knew that times spent in prayer and contemplation added to, rather than subtracted from, his ability to respond to suffering humanity. In silence, there is guidance, inspiration, and focus. In stillness, there is the inspiration to go beyond political polarization and seek common ground even with opposing viewpoints. Silence nurtures spiritual stature and energy for the long haul. Prophetic ministry is completed by listening to the still small voice that replenishes and guides us since most of the key social issues require long haul commitments and the ability to patiently endure and yet confront intransigent social and economic structures.

Roads Not Travelled. Today's reading might inspire the preacher to embody the spirit of Mark's Gospel by inviting congregants to form a healing circle for prayer and anointing after the worship service. The preacher might also investigate with the congregation whether or not God's heals persons today. The congregation might consider: Do dramatic healings occur today? What happens when people aren't healed? Does God play favorites, healing some and leaving others to die?

After church, the pastor or another key leader might give a brief course in contemplative prayer. He or she can share various meditative techniques, including breath prayer (slowing breathing in and out in a mindful fashion); visualization prayers (imaging your breath filling you with healing light); or centering prayer (focusing on a short prayer word or mantra to experience God in this holy moment).

SPIRITUAL PRACTICES
FOR THE PREACHER AND CONGREGATION

Affirmative Faith. Throughout the week, repeat these affirmations, or variations, to deepen your encounter with scripture.

> *I join prayer and action to deepen my faith.*
> *I take time for prayer and meditation.*
> *My prayers inspire me to healing actions in daily life.*

A Spiritual Practice for Preachers. At the heart of this week's practice is a spiritual examination, based on the following questions: Do you have a holy place where you go to pray or meditate? Do you set apart sacred time for prayer and meditation? If not, where and when might you focus on deepening your relationship with God?

Set aside some time to search for a deserted place for prayer and stillness.

Faith at home. This week think about creating a special prayer space in your home. It can be an underutilized room or a section of a larger room. You might set up some candles, a cross, flowers, or a photo to set this space aside from usual domestic activities.

Consider finding a particular personal time to be set aside each day for personal prayer. Can you find a similar time for the family? This may prove challenging, but you might encourage some quiet time either in the morning before school or in the evening before bed. This ritual can be quite simply:

- A time to review the day.
- A time of thanksgiving.
- A time to pray for others.
- A few moments of quiet.
- Blessing the day: either morning or evening.

Sixth Sunday After the Epiphany
Mark 1:40-45

Healing is a sign of divine love. Jesus' healing ministry is not only a demonstration of his authority over evil spirits and his unique relationship to God. It is also a revelation of God's desire for human well-being. In the spirit of the prophet Jeremiah, God has plans for us, and these plans are for good and not evil, and a future and hope. (Jeremiah 29:11) God wants us to have abundant life. But, we aren't always certain that God is on our side. We wonder if God might be the source of our illnesses or if God has somehow abandoned us.

In the first century and throughout Hebraic history, persons with skin diseases were considered social and religious outcasts. Their disease rendered them religiously unclean and unable to participate in the rites of their faith. Further, they became social non-persons: as threats to the spiritual health of the community, they could not come into contact with healthy people. They were truly God-forsaken. Moreover, their skin condition was perceived as a sign of God's punishment for their sins or a manifestation of God's will. Regardless of the cause, demon possession was a curse upon them and their families. It might reflect some sort of inherent evil disposition or possession by a malign spirit. The duration of such skin diseases might vary, but as long as persons were symptomatic, they were outcasts and pariahs. No wonder this man had second thoughts about approaching the healer Jesus. How could any holy person embrace him in his current condition? How could God care for him, especially when he had been banished from God's sight?

With hesitancy, this man approaches Jesus with a plea for healing, "If you choose, you can make me clean?" If you choose, you can restore me to my family, my profession, and my religion. If you choose, you can give me my life back!

Jesus feels this man's pain, and is inspired to respond without hesitation or ambiguity. "I do choose. Be made clean." He responds with compassion and anger at all that stands in the way of sharing in God's abundant life and full partnership in God's realm.

Persons can think of all the reasons for their illness and often these are theologically-based. These usually involve divine abandonment, an expression of divine sovereignty, or punishment for sins. All of these suggest that God is the source of the sufferings we experience. But, are these the only reasons for our suffering? What if illness arises from factors that God also opposes and wants to eradicate?

Today's scriptures invite pastors to claim their role as congregational theologians by exploring God's role in the suffering we experience. We need not be overly subtle but we can raise the key questions, "Is God on our side? Does God seek health or illness? Is God's power defined primarily by force or love?" We cannot avoid some responsibility for certain health conditions, but we are typically only partly responsible for our well-being or illness. Other factors such as environment, economics, genetics, germs, our parents' education, and family of origin significantly contribute to our overall well-being. Sometimes there is no clear reason; accidents happen. Still, we can affirm that in every life situation God is working to bring health and wholeness for ourselves and others. God's power may not be absolute but it can make a difference and elicit our partnership in our recovery and the recovery of others.

So What? Theology is practical and pastoral in nature. If we believe that God is on our side – and just as importantly on everyone's side – seeking well-being and wholeness, then we will be open to new possibilities for healing for ourselves and others. Further, in partnership with God, we are inspired to see our encounters with vulnerable persons as opportunities for compassion rather than judgment. We also need to examine our own attitudes to persons outside of our circle of relationships. How do we treat persons with serious illness, physical disfigurement, mental illness, and challenges of body, mind, and spirit? Are they non-persons to us or do we see their deepest identity as God's beloved children?

Roads Not Travelled. The preacher can focus on *our* unclean people. Who are our outcasts? Who do we see as beyond the scope of God's love? To embody this in worship, during the sermon, a poorly dressed person, made up to have a skin disease, can enter the church shouting "unclean, unclean." Members of the church can get up from their seats and shout, "Leave us alone! You don't belong here!"

Given my observations of Facebook entries, we might also have a Republican or Democratic Party leader enter the sanctuary, have them scorned, and then in the spirit of Jesus embraced lovingly.

SPIRITUAL PRACTICES
FOR THE PREACHER AND CONGREGATION

Affirmative Faith. The Apostle Paul challenged the Christian community at Rome to become spiritually, intellectually, and personally transformed. (Romans 12:2) Our images of God, along with our personal self-image, need to be transformed to help us become fully in synch with God's vision for us and the world. Consider these affirmations, or variations, as a catalyst for your personal and vocational transformation.

> *God wants to make me whole.*
> *God cleanses me from all feelings of uncleanliness and low self-esteem.*
> *In Christ, I am a new creation.*

41

A Spiritual Practice for Preachers. In this practice, take time to explore your own images of God. How do you understand God's role in healing and wholeness? What does it mean for you to affirm that God wants you to have abundant life?

Ask for God's guidance to identify and respond to one situation in your life as well as one in your community that needs healing and wholeness, and a sense of God's abundance.

Faith at Home. In the week ahead, consider how your family welcomes strangers and people from different social, racial, economic, or health situations. Talk about ways you can provide hospitality to persons who differ from you and who often suffer social stigma as racial, ethnic, sexual, or economic "others."

If you have children at home, have a frank talk about the incidence of bullying at school and other contexts. Explore honestly with your children reasons why children and youth are bullied, their own attitudes toward outsiders, and ways that those who are bullied can be welcomed.

Transfiguration Sunday
Mark 9:2-9

The celebration of Jesus' transfiguration awakens us to a new perception of our lives and the world. Mark is very realistic about Jesus' disciples. They are often totally unaware of who he is as God's beloved child and messenger. The evil spirits – along with the vulnerable and socially ostracized – know what Jesus is capable of, but the disciples, along with Jesus' own family, are often oblivious to his mission to bring healing and wholeness to the world.

For a moment, however, all of that changed: Jesus is transformed before Peter, James, and John. The light of creation shines through his cells and soul. Their eyes are opened and they see Jesus as the spiritual equal of Moses and Elijah. They hear God placing him above these spiritual giants and God's fully beloved child. In the spirit of William Blake, their "doors of perception are opened" and they see Jesus as he truly is – infinite and energetic as God's beloved child and God's "yes" to humanity. Like Isaiah in the Temple, they experience the world as full of God's glory and Jesus as the focal point of God's revelation to humankind.

Their experience is spiritually overwhelming. They are tempted to freeze their mystical encounter in time. They want to build dwelling places to insure that this moment will last forever. But, mystical experiences and divine theophanies are not intended to be the end of the journey. We pause awhile and plant our feet on holy ground, savoring the solid rock upon which we stand, but eventually we must break camp and begin the march toward Zion and Calvary's hilltop.

The Transfiguration marks a turning point in Mark's gospel. Jesus sets his face toward Jerusalem, conflict, and eventual death. Although Jesus had choices and could have bypassed Jerusalem, I believe that he chose the way of the cross as the fullest expression of his own mountaintop experience. On the mountaintop, Jesus may have felt himself transformed; he may have experienced divine power flowing through him, and felt the energy by which God created the universe as his deepest reality. Filled with divine insight and energy, he was ready to embrace whatever lay ahead for him. Though Jesus did not relish pain or the cross on the horizon, he now knew for sure that out of death, new life emerges, and God's "yes" triumphs over every human "no."

The glory of God embraces the totality of life. Experiencing God's glory leads Jesus from the mountaintop to the cross. Spiritual evolution turns us toward, not away from, the suffering of humankind. Like the Buddhist image of the bodhisattva, Jesus lets go of his glory – of the wondrous energy of transfiguration – to save struggling humankind. Our own spiritual practices share in this same embodiment. They connect us with the energy of the universe and fill us with radical amazement. They also inspire us to become God's partners in healing the world.

So What? The transfiguration of Jesus seems irrelevant to our daily lives. In what way can a dazzling Jesus be of help to us? Jesus' identity as set apart from humankind and filled with divine light is interesting, but not inherently life-changing. Unless…and it is a big unless, we find our own lives and world transformed. Transfiguration reminds us of the infinite wonder of life and invites us to slow down for a moment to experience the infinity of each moment. Annie Dillard speaks of seeing a dazzling light shining through the trees as pivotal spiritual moment and invites us to ponder our own "tree with lights." Moses encounters a burning bush on his way to work, and stops long enough to hear God's vision for his life. Still, awestruck and shoeless, Moses must put his shoes back on to fulfill his vocation as his peoples' liberator. Mysticism always leads to movement; not frenetic movement, but steps guided by divine wisdom and compassion.

Roads Not Travelled. Today's reading calls for a light show, lively music, and flashing lights. It invites dancing and singing to "We are Marching in the Light of God" (Siyahamba). Perhaps, the preacher can lead in a dance around the worship space.

SPIRITUAL PRACTICES
FOR THE PREACHER AND CONGREGATION

Affirmative Faith. Transfiguration leads to a transformed perception of the world. Although moments of transfiguration happen unexpectedly and often without our efforts, spiritual practices, including affirmations, awaken us to God's dazzling light in ourselves and in everyone we meet.

God's light shines in all things. God's light shines in me.
God's dazzling light is my deepest reality.
I see God's light shining in everyone I meet.

A Spiritual Practice for Preachers. In this practice, we join silence with holy imagination. We begin with a time of silence, breathing deeply and slowly, and opening to God's enlivening breath. After several moments of gentle breathing, begin to visualize a healing light (of a color of your choice) filling you with each breath, starting at the top of the head and gently flowing toward your toes. Let God's light fill you fully and completely.

After a few minutes, visualize a friend or family member. With each breath, imagine that person filled with God's inspiring and healing light. Let that common light surround and protect you.

Faith at Home. People of all ages can experience God's dazzling, healing, transforming light. Children are natural mystics, whose worlds are filled with wonder and whose imaginations open them to alternate realities. We need to integrate the wisdom and skills of maturity with the wonder and imagination of youth. We can experience burning bushes and transfigurations everywhere if we open the doors of perception to divine illumination.

In this practice, we join silence with holy imagination. We begin with a time of silence, breathing deeply and slowly, and opening to God's enlivening breath. After several moments of gentle breathing, begin to visualize a healing light (of a color of your choice) filling you with each breath, starting at the top of the head and gently flowing toward your toes. Let God's light fill you fully and completely.

After a few minutes, visualize a friend or family member. With each breath, imagine that person filled with God's inspiring and healing light. Let that common light surround and protect you both.

Seventh Sunday after the Epiphany
Mark 2:1-12

Healing takes many forms, whether it involves medication or meditation, anointing or anesthesia, forgiveness or pharmaceuticals. Mark's healing journey continues with the multidimensional healing of a paralyzed man. Jesus' attempt to keep his powers secret is an utter failure. When he returns to his home in Capernaum, he discovers that his home is surrounded by a crowd of supplicants, urgently awaiting his healing touch. His home becomes a makeshift tabernacle for teaching and healing. Still, some are unable to gain access to the healer.

As the day unfolds, four men carry their friend to see Jesus. They discover that the pathway to healing is blocked. At this juncture, they could have given up and taken their friend home. But, they persist. Perhaps, they see the situation as the *kairos,* "now or never," moment. If they give up now, their friend will always be an invalid, dependent on the generosity of others. So, they do the socially and legally unthinkable, they climb up to the roof and tear a hole in the healer's roof to gain access to Jesus.

We don't know how the paralyzed man felt. Did he protest their actions? Did he come reluctantly or with expectation? As the straw and mud fall into Jesus' room, the healer gazes upward at the friends and the man being lowered through the roof. "When Jesus saw their faith, he said to the paralytic, 'Son, your sins are forgiven.'" The curious reader might ask, "To whom is Jesus referring – the man with paralysis, the whole group, or just the four friends?"

This healing story reveals several aspects of the healing journey, applicable to many peoples' quests for wholeness. First, when we see healing and personal transformation for ourselves and others, we often face obstacles. Healing is not straight forward, formulaic, or easy. It may take persistence, patience, and the willingness to live with unanswered prayer and our own or others' personal blocks to healing. Second, healing involves a community as well as individuals. We all need companions on the healing journey, whose faith in God and us is stronger than our faith in ourselves. Sometimes when we lack faith, we need to rely on the faith of others who believe on our behalf. Third, there is a relationship between forgiveness and healing. Jesus' encounter with the paralyzed man should not be generalized as an explanation for all forms of illness. Sickness can be the result of behaviors and attitudes; it can also result from random causes, diet, DNA, and environmental factors.

The story concludes with an affirmation that Jesus has the authority to transform cells as well as souls. When we find ourselves in synch with God's healing energy, we may experience wonders and proclaim in our own time, "We have never seen anything like this!"

So What? This story portrays the many dimensions of healing and illness. It calls us to consider who we would reach out to if we were in physical, spiritual, or emotional duress. It also challenges us to consider persons for whom we might serve as healing companions. Further, as an examination of conscience, we might reflect on what stands in the way of our own personal healing.

Roads Not Travelled. Dare the pastor pronounce forgiveness on the congregation? Dare he or she ask the congregation to quietly name their secret sins, write them on a piece of paper, and then deposit them into a crucible to be burned? This sermon can be acted out after a conversation about what the congregants would do if someone was so desperate to get into the church that he or she broke a window or forced a door.

SPIRITUAL PRACTICES
FOR THE PREACHER AND CONGREGATION

Affirmative Faith. The use of affirmations awakens the healing power resident in our cells and souls. God is constantly seeking our healing; affirmations help us respond to God's call to wholeness.

> *I accept the help of others in my healing process.*
> *I reach out to others when I need help.*
> *I persist in spite of difficulties and challenges.*

A Spiritual Practice for Preachers. Many pastors, including this writer, struggle with accepting the help of others. We believe that we have the resources to make it on our own. We fail to reach out to others out of pride, independence, and feelings of self-sufficiency. Yet, when we reach out to trusted friends and colleagues, we often find the support we need to face our personal and professional difficulties. The story of paralyzed man reminds us of the importance of confidential and supportive colleague groups for clergy. Many denominations and counseling centers provide professional support groups. You may also choose to initiate an informal colleague group of pastors in your area, if no external resources are available.

Faith at Home. The story of the man with paralysis reminds us that it takes a village to bring healing to individuals and families. Around the table, reflect on people your family feels called to pray for. Conversely, think about supportive friends to whom each member might go if he or she is facing difficulties. (Of course, children and youth should, first of all, seek the help of parents, grandparents, and school officials. But, are there other safe and supportive adults to whom they can turn in case of trouble?)

47

Eighth Sunday after the Epiphany
Mark 2:13-22

Healing involves spirit as well as body. The call of Levi involves what John Biersdorf describes as the healing of purpose. As I imagine the encounter of Levi and Jesus, I visualize a history between the two very different men: over the past several weeks, Levi and Jesus have gotten to know one another. Jesus may have engaged Levi in conversation, raising issues of faith in a way the tax collector had not experienced in his adult life. In fact, Levi might not have had a spiritual conversation with a fellow Jew after he began to collect taxes for the Roman occupation force. He was considered dishonest, unclean, and an outcast, and although Levi was no doubt affluent by comparison to his fellow Jews, his affluence could not buy friendship, respect, or entrée into polite society and the synagogue community. Unlike others, Jesus may have treated Levi with respect. Jesus prepared the ground for further conversation by treating Levi as a beloved child of God. Perhaps, Jesus explored questions of meaning and happiness with Levi, not telling, but asking, "Are you happy? Do you feel fulfilled? What are you planning to do with the rest of your life?" At the right time, the *kairos* moment, Jesus posed the question, "Follow me," and Levi followed, leaving a life of financial security for an uncertain but fulfilling adventure of the spirit.

Like another tax collector, Zacchaeus, Levi found himself hosting Jesus for dinner. "Be careful who you eat with" was a slogan prized in Jesus' community. The religion police can't imagine Jesus eating with a group of tax collectors and social outcasts. Yet, the physician of the spirit looks deeper into his patients than his righteous critics. The righteous are insulated from their sense of sin and inadequacy by their "goodness." They need God's grace, but their assumed goodness stands in the way of their receiving it. On the other hand, those who are sick recognize their neediness. They perceive their alienation from society and distance from God. They know that, despite their affluence, they are far from God's realm and they can't make it without God's help. Like persons in recovery, they know that only the grace of a higher power can deliver them from alienation and addiction.

Jesus' ministry falls outside the realm of propriety. His followers bend the rules, celebrate, and color outside the lines of orthodoxy. Religion as usual cannot contain the wine of the spirit. Jesus' new vision requires new words, practices, and institutions. The "new" can contain the old wine of tradition, but traditionalism is unable to contain the freedom of God's realm.

So What? Jarislav Pelikan once noted the tradition is the living thoughts of dead people, while traditionalism is the dead thoughts of living people. What dead thoughts and practices constrain your congregation? What old ways of life threaten the new life in Christ that calls your congregation forward? How might Christ be born in new ways in your congregation? What do you need to make new wine and wineskins for your congregation?

Roads Not Travelled. The preacher can publically name the dead traditions that plague the church and her or his own congregation. Like Ezekiel, he can ask, "Can these dry bones live?" and listen for the answer within the congregation. If the answer is "yes," what must the congregation do to come alive again?

SPIRITUAL PRACTICES
FOR THE PREACHER AND CONGREGATION

Affirmative Faith. Today's scripture calls us to embrace novelty and otherness, and to expand our personal, ethical, and spiritual comfort zones.

> *I welcome outsiders as God's beloved children.*
> *I embrace new behaviors to be faithful to God.*
> *I see God's presence in all of its unexpected disguises.*

A Spiritual Practice for Preachers. Jesus proclaimed that as you have done unto the least of these, you have done unto me. Jesus Christ, the beloved child of God, experiences the joy and pain of creation. In this practice, simply take a moment to experience the divine presence in everyone you meet. You may choose to quietly or internally invoke your awareness with phrases such as: "God bless you," "The Spirit in Me Greets the Spirit in You," "I greet you as Christ."

Faith at Home. Family life is a crucible for spiritual formation. Our greatness kindness and most fierce moments of antipathy often occur under the same roof. In this practice, begin by choosing to experience the divine presence in everyone in your family. You may choose to quietly or internally invoke your awareness with phrases such as: "God bless you," "The Spirit in Me Greets the Spirit in You," "I greet you as Christ." Let these blessings transmit to caring behaviors. Encourage family members to go beyond the family to share these same affirmations with people you meet in the course of the day.

Ninth Sunday after the Epiphany
Mark 2:23-3:6

Today's reading takes us beyond our theological, religious, and cultural comfort zones. Our familiar practices can take on a life of their own. The practice becomes everything and persons have to conform to the practice and ritual even it isn't helpful to them. Abstract rules and liturgical and cultural habits can take precedence over real human experience and the healing of persons.

Order is essential for creativity and routines are necessary for a properly organization, family, or personal life, but these are intended to support, rather than restrict, our creativity, innovation, and compassion. Even practices embedded in our religious history, such as the Sabbath, need to be relativized in light of human well-being. "The Sabbath was made for humankind, and not humankind for the Sabbath."

Still, we can affirm the inherent value of certain religious practices, held flexibly and open to revision. Sabbath-keeping is essential to human well-being. Sadly, our technological culture, and even church culture, have not only relativized the Sabbath, but essentially relegated the Sabbath to an era piece, subservient to convenience, profit-making, and busyness. An insightful pastor would invite his congregants to explore their cultural and religious inflexibilities, while affirming the importance of Sabbath-keeping in the spiritual journey. The key question is: In what ways does

Sabbath-keeping contribute to human well-being? How can we practice Sabbath in a technological society? Ironically, today, we are as inflexible about our need to be in touch technologically and digitally as earlier religious leaders were about Sabbath-keeping. Today, we might ask: Is the technology made for humankind or humankind for technology? Does our technology serve us or do we become the servants of the tools intended to streamline our lives?

Jesus' admonition against religious inflexibility is embodied in the healing of man with a withered hand. With the religious teachers lying in wait, ready to criticize him, Jesus asks, "Is it lawful to do good or harm on the Sabbath?" The answer is clear, and the religious leaders remain silent. Again, we are met with a multilayered healing story. The relief of pain and the empowerment of those suffering from physical illness ought to be unambiguous, regardless of time or place. Jesus invites the man into a healing partnership: Jesus calls and the man responds; he stretches out his hand, opening to God's energy of healing. Healing and wholeness of persons and institutions is the result of a dynamic call and response in which we answer the call of God, opening to the abundant life God has planned for us.

So What? Today's reading invites us to explore our personal and congregational inflexibilities. Where do our practices enhance God's presence and where do they stand in the way of faithfulness to God? Moreover, this passage invites us to explore ways we can practice Sabbath-time as persons and congregations.

Roads Not Travelled. Many preachers would stir up a hornet's nest if they invited their congregants to consider the following flexible adjustments to their lifestyle: 1) an internet Sabbath and 2) a sabbatical from kid's sports on Sunday mornings. Over the past two decades, Sunday worship and faith formation has had to compete with weekend sports, and sadly in many churches, parents have chosen sports over spirituality. Sports are not antithetical to spirituality, let me be clear, but our motivations for sports typically involve winning in the now and imagining the possibility of a college scholarship in the future. Sunday sports seldom aim at character building from my experience as a coach and player. Just as heretical is the notion that we will go off line for several hours to spend the afternoon in conversation with friends and family members, playing games, relaxing, praying, and reading devotional literature. It's a matter of commitment and time allocation.

While I do not make a strict differentiation between Christ and culture, I believe the church needs to have a complementary and guiding role, and not a subservient role, to the many activities in which our children and youth are involved. We should also see our congregation's programs for youth and children as serious and requiring commitment. Lacking the threat of hell, many churches present few good reasons why participation in their programs is just as important as Sunday sports.

SPIRITUAL PRACTICES
FOR THE PREACHER AND CONGREGATION

Affirmative Faith. Affirmations invite us to re-imagine our practices and way of life. This week's affirmations open us to become partners in God's compassionate creativity.

I stretch out my hand to receive God's blessings.
I take time to rest and reflect.
I balance action and contemplation.

A Spiritual Practice for Preachers. While many of us cling to inflexible rules and practices, one of the greatest challenges ministers face is letting go of our need to be on duty 24/7. We are constantly available, checking our e-mail, texting, and responding to phone calls. We go from one event to another, and often fail to experience any coherent pattern or meaning to our lives. We need to follow the counsel of the Psalmist and "pause awhile" and remember God's presence. (Psalm 46:10)

Take time for a pastoral Sabbath, a regular time each week for refreshment, reading, and restoration. There is no one type of Sabbath: the main issue is to make a commitment to practices that restore your mind, body, and spirit.

Faith at Home. Explore a family Sabbath for a few hours each week. There is no one style of Sabbath, but some elements

52

might include a leisurely meal, a walk, games, sporting activities, or rest. For a few hours turn off the television, unplug the phone, and turn off the internet. Embrace the simple joys of life. Talk to your family about your values and how your commitments might align with them.

THE SEASON OF LENT:
SEEKING SIMPLICITY

The motto for Lent could be "I am the vine you are the branches, connected to me you will bear much fruit." (John 15:5) Lent challenges us to prune away everything that stands in the way of God's energy and inspiration flowing in and through us.

When I was interim pastor of a congregation near Hagerstown, Maryland, I once asked a farmer why he pruned his apple trees. He smiled and said, "To let the light in." Lenten pruning is intended to let God's light shine in our lives so that we might share that light with others. Mark's Jesus is fully human, translucent and transparent to the divine. He calls us to repent, turn around, prune the inessential, so we can experience God's good news and let God's light shine to give light to the world.

Mark's Jesus experiences temptations, but brings everything back to God. He knows that he can't do it alone, so he constantly undergirds his ministry with prayer and meditation. He goes where the wild things are, and the wildest place of all is the human spirit. We, like Jesus, need God's angelic presence to guide and protect us in the temptations of life. Spiritual growth plunges us into intricate independence of life in which we are always receiving, mostly unnoticed blessings from the world around us, and then can bless others out of our spiritual and material abundance.

The First Sunday in Lent
Mark 1:9-15

This week's readings present a holy trinity of interdependent preaching possibilities: the baptism of Jesus; his retreat in the wilderness; and the initiation of his public ministry.

In our Bible study on Mark's Gospel at South Congregational Church, where I serve as pastor, one of the participants asked, "Why did Jesus have to be baptized? He was the Son of God, wasn't he? He didn't need to repent or confess his sins,

54

did he?" She had a good point, and the best answer is "we don't know." Not knowing, however, can be the inspiration to faithful agnosticism and holy imagination.

As I move from text to imagination, I believe Jesus' baptism could have, first of all, been signal that the time to begin his public ministry was imminent. It was time to put all his study and prayer into practice, to come out as God's beloved teacher and healer, and this was the *kairos* moment, the public entry point that would define his vocation as God's teacher, healer, and savior. And what an entry point it was! The heavens open, a dove descends, and God's voice booms like thunder, "You are my beloved son." Was Jesus' baptism a quantum leap in his own spiritual formation? Did he receive new power from heaven? Did he finally truly know the nature of his life mission? Mark's descent of the Spirit seems to fill Jesus with power and propel him into the wilderness for reflection.

Jesus' baptism also affirms his continuity with us. Jesus is fully human, and fully alive. He is one of us, flesh and blood, hungry and thirsty, energized and weary, and even tempted to turn from his highest good. There is no separate human part and divine part in Jesus; in Jesus, divinity and humanity meet in a fully embodied historical human being. He is one of us, fully and completely, and in sharing our lives, he brings the possibility of healing to every human condition.

Jesus has little time to enjoy his apotheosis. He is immediately, and Mark loves the word "immediately," driven into the wilderness by God's Spirit. We have hints of the Holy Trinity here, and the presence of the Spirit as the voice of God, guiding and illuminating our pathway. The Spirit lures Jesus forward to a spiritual retreat in the wilderness. Far from the hustle and bustle of human busyness, Jesus can take time to reflect on his mission. Yet, in silence, we often hear voices of temptation and inner conflict. In the sparseness of Mark's description, we learn on the bare facts that Jesus is tempted by Satan. We have no idea about the nature of these temptations, or how Jesus responded. These are elaborated in Matthew 4:1-11 and Luke 4:1-13. But, we do know that our greatest gifts can be the source of our greatest temptations. The fully human Jesus experiences the attraction of the roads he must avoid if he is to fulfill his destiny as God's beloved one, our teacher and savior.

Jesus was free to choose his path. His spiritual adventure was open-ended and depended on his own choice and creativity.

Many people think that following God's way means strict obedience to a predetermined path and that any deviation is a fall from grace. While error and sin may emerge from deviations from God's highest possibilities, there is also the deviation born of creativity, innovation, and faithfulness. I believe Jesus models for us the many paths of faithfulness, emerging from God's moment by moment and long-term visions for our lives. In each moment, God presents us with possibilities and the energy to embody them; God leaves the actual embodiment to us, affirming that our incarnation of God's vision is a result of our own openness to grace. Perhaps, God, like an open-spirited parent says to us, "Do something new! Alter my design! Show me what you can do! Surprise me!"

The wilderness is the place "where the wild things are" and Jesus is accompanied by wild beasts. Did these beasts threaten Jesus? Or, did the one who could calm a storm have such resonance with the non-human world that the beasts became friendly, protecting Jesus from harm and providing him with nourishment?

In the wilderness, Jesus is not alone. Angelic beings minister to him, providing for his needs. We, too, must go to the wilderness of life, eventually, and that wilderness can be a time of spiritual discernment, relational conflict, physical illness, or dying. In the wilderness, we may discover nourishment and care from angelic beings, both human and non-human, including the wild beasts we once feared.

The scripture ends with Jesus going public in his ministry. John's arrest leaves a spiritual void that only Jesus can fill. Now is the time for preaching good news! Now is the time for God's realm to take shape in human life. Like John, Jesus calls the people to turn around and take a new spiritual and relational pathway. He also challenges them to believe in the gospel, the good news, of God's realm.

Mark is vague about the nature of the "good news," but surely Jesus' ministry is the embodiment of his opening message. Believe in the good news: God welcomes you; you have a home in God's realm regardless of your past or social standing; God wants you to be free of all illness and forms of possession; God is on your side and will do everything possible for you to claim your own place as God's beloved child.

Lent is a season of simplicity and contemplation. It is a time for pruning the extraneous. The Lenten disciplines are a prelude to celebration and the joy of companionship in God's holy adventure of Shalom.

So What? Today's scriptures remind us that the worst temptation is to think you have no temptation. Jesus is "everywoman" and "everyman" in his wilderness retreat. His retreat invites us to listen to our lives, as Frederick Buechner advises, as a prelude to letting our life speak (Parker Palmer) in actions that are intended to bring joy and healing to those around us. Going to the wilderness invites us to face our addictions, especially the socially acceptable and subtle ones (busyness, indispensability, co-dependence, success and perfectionism) as well as the more obviously destructive addictive behaviors. We are reminded that we are never alone and that God gives us resources in the form of wise persons, helpful institutions, and the collective wisdom and faith of the body of Christ.

As model for our own spiritual journeys, Jesus invites us to embody "good news" in our daily lives. What is the good news we will share with our children, parents, co-workers, fellow Christians, and larger community? The world needs good news as an antidote to our addiction to negativity and polarization.

Roads Not Travelled. The adventurous preacher might go in a few wild and crazy directions. First, he or she might let the first Sunday in Lent be an opportunity to reflect on the reality of angels. Despite the many accounts of angels in scripture, angels are seldom invoked in mainstream and progressive sermons. Accompanied by paintings of angels, ancient and modern, the preacher might muse on the significance of angels in the religious journey. Second, the preacher might explore the wild things, considering what companion animals might be both threatening and supportive in our spiritual journey. What totem animal might reflect the highest spirit of the congregation and its mission?

SPIRITUAL PRACTICES
FOR THE PREACHER AND CONGREGATION

Affirmative Faith. Today's affirmations open us to living God's good news in daily life. Repeat throughout the day, these affirmations, or ones of your choice.

> *I am God's beloved child and God loves me.*
> *God is with me in times of temptation.*
> *I share God's good news wherever I go.*

A Spiritual Practice for Preachers. Many preachers take their sermons out for a walk. This morning, as I was preparing for a meeting at the United Church of Christ national office in Cleveland, Ohio, I began the day reading Mark 1:9-15. I then took off on a forty five minute walk through downtown Cleveland and down to the lakeshore, taking time for prayer and letting the words of this scripture soak in. I returned to my hotel and with pen and paper, let the insights flow.

Take time to go out for a preacher's walk as you prepare for your sermon. Read the scripture a few times with pauses in between, and then let your mind wander as you walk through your neighborhood, a place of beauty, or in the vicinity of the church. Let the images and ideas flow without any judgment. When you return to your home or study, take a few minutes to write your ideas down as you free associate. "God is still speaking," as the United Church of Christ motto affirms, and God is speaking within your heart and mind as you walk along with the scriptures as your companions.

Faith at Home. As a family, take time to share what you think "good news" might mean in your family life, school, or workplace. How can you share good news? What good news might you wish to share? Make a commitment to share good news around the house by the way you treat each other and the words you use. Let this same commitment include your interactions at school and work. Close this time of reflection with a time of thanksgiving for the opportunity to be a voice of love and affirmation in the world.

The Second Sunday in Lent
Mark 8:31-38 and/or Mark 9:2-9

The God described in Mark's Gospel is keenly aware of our suffering. The first ten chapters of Mark describe in greater detail than any other gospel Jesus' concern for healing body, mind, spirit, and relationships. Jesus is the compassionate one, who feels our pain, and reflects the intimacy of philosopher Alfred North Whitehead's description of God as the "fellow sufferer who understands."

This Sunday recalls both Jesus' suffering and glory. The wise preacher can choose one or the other, or join the join the two scriptures as two sides of the same reality. The one who suffers and asks us to take up our cross is also the one who is glorified by God's all-healing power. The one whose transfiguration reflects the very creative power of the universe, the energy of the big bang and fourteen billion years of evolution, also intimately shares our human condition in all its joy and sorrow, moving through our cells and souls to bring about God's realm of Shalom.

The Son of God must suffer! Take up your cross and follow me! If you deny the realities of suffering and avoid them at all costs, you will have forfeited, at least for the time being, the fullness of God's realm.

The cross is on the horizon. Although Jesus has choices and can choose to bypass Jerusalem, his destiny calls him forward, risking death to be true to God. We, too, must take risks to be faithful. This is a hard passage, in part, because we do our best to manage risk and to assess cost and benefit. We want to avoid physical and emotional pain whenever possible. Often, others' sorrows are simply too much to bear. Followers of Jesus, however, must be willing to embrace suffering for the greater good of others and to follow God's call.

Spirituality deals with what cannot be avoided, life's unfixables and the necessary losses, as noted by Alan Jones and Judith Viorst respectively, that are part of the human experience, including a good life. Choosing to avoid pain may lead to a famine of celebrating and experiencing God's presence in the least of these. The traditional marriage vows spell this out. Couples make commitments for a future that is unknown:

For better, for worse,
For richer, for poorer,
In sickness and in health.

This is the same commitment we implicitly make to our children and other loved ones. I will be here for you, taking on your suffering, sacrificing for your well-being, regardless of the cost.

Those who try to hold onto to their lives, and who cling to their separate ego and its needs, will ultimately lose their lives. Those who let go of the shrunken, individualistic self will grow in stature, connected with all creation. They will lose the frightened, acquisitive, ever-vigilant and protective self, and discover an undying, always open-spirited self. This is the vision of the body of Christ, where our joys and sorrows are one. We will feel more pain when we are connected intimately with others, and when their well-being is as important as our own, but we will also experience more joy and the peace that surpasses understanding as our own heart beats to the rhythm of the Heartbeat of the Universe.

Jesus' mountaintop glory propels him to the cross and the controversies and betrayals to come. On the mountaintop, Jesus' spiritual body bursts forth, illuminated and enlightened, a quantum body sharing in the creative power of the universe. Jesus is, as the author John's Gospel was to say a generation or two later, the light of the world and in that moment God's true light shines forth from the teacher from Nazareth. Jesus is part of a tradition of light bearers: Elijah and Moses prepared the ground and shared God's light in their time. Jesus' transfiguration is neither anomalous nor supernatural; it is of one piece with the wisdom of Jesus' Hebraic parents. As we ponder Jesus' transfiguration, we are challenged to reflect on the transfiguration of suffering through God's grace and our commitment to share in Jesus' ministry.

So What? Today's passage invites congregants to experience both wonder and suffering. The transfiguration is an invitation to open our eyes to beauty right where we are. We don't need to go to heaven or away to the beach or mountains to experience a "holy day." God's holidays are right here for those with eyes to see and ears to hear.

The wonder of life is intimately connected with our ability to experience our own and others' sufferings. Pain announces to us that what we experience matters; and turning away from pain means turning away from God. Pain is a reality that cannot be fully extinguished, but open-hearted compassion that comes from a commitment to the whole of life inspires us to be healing companions of those who suffer and to minimize unjust and unnecessary suffering. In opening Christ's invitation to lose your life, we are invited to ask ourselves questions such as:

> What causes us to close our hearts to others?
> Where are we currently experiencing the suffering of others?
> What do these encounters with suffering bring up for us emotionally and spiritually?
> What can we do to be God's partners in remedying suffering?
> Where are we called to eliminate or minimize suffering?

These questions can lead to a call to commitment and a transfiguration of values. They may lead congregants to consider their own economic values, with concern to whether they are spirit-destroying or spirit-enriching.

Roads Not Travelled. The adventurous preacher can label his sermon, "following Jesus can be dangerous to your health." He or she might also consider "death to self" as a prelude to look beyond the ego to God's vision for our lives and world.

SPIRITUAL PRACTICES
FOR THE PREACHER AND CONGREGATION

Affirmative Faith. Affirmations awaken us to the tragic beauty of life. Take time to live with these affirmations throughout the week:

> *God is constantly transfiguring and illuminating my life.*
> *I open my heart to the joy and sorrow of life.*
> *I see God's brightness in every person and situation.*

A Spiritual Practice for Preachers. Throughout the week, take time either by reading the newspaper, on-line resources, or television and radio news to reflect on the suffering of life. What tragic events touch your heart? What calls you to prayer? What might inspire action?

Remember through your compassion and the compassion of your congregation, you can be the answer to someone's prayer. As I reflect on the reality of suffering, I am struggling to comprehend the kidnapping of young girls in Nigeria, the civil war between Shiites and Sunnis in Iraq, and the realities of drug abuse, homelessness, and alcoholism on beautiful Cape Cod, and friends facing chronic and incurable illnesses. My heart is touched and I am called to respond in ways that bring healing to the world and my community with both prayer and action.

Faith at Home. During the Lenten season, reflect as a family on what you might sacrifice to be more faithful to Christ and to bring beauty and healing to those who suffer. If you choose to sacrifice an activity such as going to a movie or a dinner out, contribute the cost to a national or local charity, committed to bringing wholeness and a better life to those in need. For example, you might make a contribution to Church World Service disaster relief programs, Habitat for Humanity, Heifer Project, or the local soup kitchen. Instead of going out, you might make a casserole for a soup kitchen or homeless shelter in your community. Explore how you might do this on a more regular basis.

Sacrificial living affirms the solidarity of life and awakens your heart to greater joy and compassion.

THE HOLIEST WEEK:
GOD'S SUFFERING LOVE

The emotional and spiritual roller coaster of holy week challenges us to consider our images of God. Is God aloof and distant, swooping in to save select chosen ones? Is God immune from suffering, viewing the tragedies of our lives from a distance? Or is God truly with us in joy and sorrow? Does God understand our challenges and failures to live out the gospel? Does God feel our pain?

Mark's Jesus is fully human and fully alive and that means living through the joys and tragedies of life. Mark's Jesus, God's beloved one, reveals that the cross touches the heart of God. God is there in the suffering, forsakenness, abandonment, and death, whether on Calvary, in a militarized zone, a dysfunctional and violent family, or hospice. Truly, as Dietrich Bonhoeffer asserts, only a suffering God can save!

Mark's Jesus is also the earthly reflection of that suffering God, who heals through divine tears and confronts evil with the unbeatable power of persistent suffering love and infinite compassionate joy.

Liturgy of the Palms
Mark 1:1-11

Life in its fullness involves both celebration and lament. As Jesus and his followers enter Jerusalem to begin what was later known as Holy Week, the air is thick with tension. Something dramatic is about to happen but Jesus' followers can't fully fathom what lies ahead for them and their teacher. They have heard Jesus' cryptic comments about suffering, but have done their best to place them in the background. The idea that their teacher could suffer and die was too much to comprehend.

With darkness on the horizon the disciples spend one last day of celebration with Jesus. At Jesus' request, they secure a donkey, the symbol of peace, to transport their teacher into the city.

63

As Jesus rides into the city, he is met with adulation. He is Jerusalem's king for a moment, but he is a very different kind of king from Caesar. The crowds shout "hosanna" – save us, praise God - with abandon, affirming the joyful sovereignty of God over all that would threaten humankind.

We need moments of celebration as well as desolation. Holy Week embraces life in all its seasons – celebration, conflict, uncertainty, abandonment and suffering, death, grief, and unexpected deliverance and new life. But, today, we celebrate!

We don't know anything about the Palm Sunday revelers. Did they stick with Jesus to the end? Were they simply caught up in the excitement of the moment, unaware of the true nature of Jesus' ministry? Did some of them end up joining the crowd calling to crucify Jesus a few short days later?

Palm Sunday compels us to examine our own fidelity. This is a question we hate to ask ourselves and it certainly might sound offensive if we asked it in our congregations: What is our breaking point? What would push us from celebration to abandonment? Very few of us make any significant sacrifice for being Christians in North America. In fact, for many following Jesus is just one activity among many, fitting into our life along with kids' soccer practice, dinner parties, hobbies, and sports. Being a Christian can be good for business, as suggested by the Christian Yellow Pages, and can enhance our love life and find us a good spouse as advertised by Christian Mingle. In principle, there is nothing wrong with such enterprises, except when they portray faith as a barter and guarantee of good fortune, romance, and financial success. For the first century followers of Jesus, there were no such guarantees. Though they were citizens of God's eternal realm, they first had to travel through the valley of the shadow of death.

So What? The celebrations of Palm Sunday challenge us to explore ways that we can ground our moments of spiritual ecstasy in long term commitment. How do we join emotional fervor with long-haul fidelity?

Roads Not Travelled. Seize the moment for celebration for tomorrow we die! Adventures of the spirit are tragic comedies, but today we celebrate the triumphant Christ. There will be enough suffering between now and Easter morning. Blow horns, bring a donkey to church, launch balloons, shoot off fireworks, and eat hearty. Whole-life faith is ecstatic and joyful and also filled with authentic grief and tears. Don't let your hosannas be half-hearted, nor your laments and grief be muted.

SPIRITUAL PRACTICES
FOR THE PREACHER AND CONGREGATION

Affirmative Faith. Pastors have a difficult week ahead. Holy Week is filled with extra services as well as the demands of home visits. Everything needs to be just so for Easter! Like the first followers of Jesus, pastors need to find ways to ground the frenetic activity of Holy Week and Easter in moments of calm contemplation. Affirmations can enable us to find a quiet center amid the busiest congregational weeks.

> *I balance action and contemplation in my ministry and personal life.*
> *Peace is just a breath away.*
> *I have all the time and energy I need to faithfully serve God at church, in the world, and at home.*

A Spiritual Practice for Preachers. Vietnamese Buddhist monk Thich Nhat Hanh says that peace is every step. In this spiritual practice, I invite you to walk your prayers. Take a few minutes at least twice a day for a walking break. You may choose to walk slowly and deliberately or at a fast pace. But, as you walk, take time to breathe deeply, visualizing God's Spirit filling you with energy, calm, and insight with every breath.

Faith at Home. Consider adapted the aforementioned spiritual practice for preachers. Take time for walking prayer, opening to God's Spirit with each breath. Enjoy opening to go as you move your body and let your senses awaken God's good earth. Later, around the table, take time to talk about what it means to celebrate Jesus' presence in your life. Consider the temptations to falling away from the way of Jesus.

65

Liturgy of Christ's Passion
Mark 14:1-15:47

A traditional spiritual asks, "Were you there when they crucified my Lord?" and, then, suggests that the only appropriate answer is "yes." We were there and are still there. The Passion of Christ is about the whole of our lives: our fidelity and betrayal; our courage and cowardice; our celebration and desolation. There are revelations of love and violence, and senseless acts of love and beauty. Even in the midst of conflict, with a cross on the horizon, beauty is never gratuitous. It touches the heart of God and gives meaning to our swiftly passing lives.

The passionate Christ is fully human: he could have avoided the cross, prayed for the possibility of a different path; instead, he followed God's vision. Jesus followed his destiny, not a predetermined path, and his vocation led him to Jerusalem, conflict, and the cross.

The passion of the Christ also invokes the quiet power of powerlessness. The woman at the cross can do nothing, but they can love their teacher and friend, and their love echoes through the ages, reminding us that the dying above all need our care, whether on Calvary's cross, in the streets of Calcutta, or a cancer ward.

The finality of death overwhelms us with loss and grief. The end of Jesus is abrupt, the dead end, the end of a face to face relationship, and yet perhaps the beginning of a new holy adventure in God's care.

So What? The passion of Jesus challenges us to consider our fidelity and our breaking point. Are we now betraying Jesus? What would cause us to move from fidelity to betrayal? What temptations lure us away from God's realm? What crosses are we called to bear and witness? How shall we respond to the crosses of others?

Roads Not Travelled. An adventurous preacher might portray the passion of Jesus through the experiences of Jesus and others who were present during Holy Week: the woman who anointed Jesus; Peter; Jesus' in the garden; the women at the cross; Joseph of Arimathea.

SPIRITUAL PRACTICES
FOR THE PREACHER AND CONGREGATION

Affirmative Faith. Can we live affirmatively in times of crisis? Though essentially positive, our affirmations can also awaken us to the tragedies of life.

> *I am open-hearted and embrace the joys and sorrows of life.*
> *I reach out to anoint with God's spirit persons in crisis.*
> *I reach out to care by prayers and actions those who are facing death.*

A Spiritual Practice for Preachers. In the midst of holy week, we need to stop a moment for prayer and meditation. Pause amid the busyness of the week to breathe deeply God's care, and experience God's healing touch, so that we can go through holy week with compassion and love.

Faith at Home. The holy week stories may be too graphic for young children. In your family spiritual formation, make time to talk about persons in need and how your family can bring baskets of love along with Easter baskets. Talk about how sacrificing for others can bring them joy and you greater happiness.

EASTER SEASON:
NEW LIFE ABOUNDS

Mark's Easter is spare. There are no seaside encounters, on the road adventures, encounters in the garden, or passing through walls in the first edition of the earliest gospel. The original ending of Mark doesn't even have an embodied Jesus. There is an open future in which Jesus goes ahead of his disciples and us, gently preparing us for whatever future awaits us in this life and in God's realm. Followers of Jesus must go forward to find him; letting go of their previous images to embrace further adventures with God's beloved one.

Easter Morning
Mark 16:1-8

He is not here! Jesus is going ahead of you! Mark's resurrection story – the original story – gives the barest description of an event that transforms history and gives birth to the Christian movement. We encounter an angel but no wounds, healing breaths, quiet garden encounters, or meals on the lakeshore.

Mark's beginnings and endings are equally stark. Just as there is no virgin birth, nor is there a description of the Risen Jesus. But, what we experience is an open, unfettered, and unlimited future.

The story begins with lament and tragedy. Mary, Mary Magdalene, and Salome journey to the tomb to pay their last respects to their beloved healer and teacher. They are worried that even this one last act of love may be denied them. "Who will roll away the stone for us from the entrance to the tomb?" To their amazement, the stone has already been rolled away, and Jesus is missing. An angel reassures them, reminding them that everything is alright; there is no need to be afraid; and that the future that lies ahead of you in God's hands.

Resurrection opens the door to the future and invites us on a holy adventure with the Risen Jesus. Like the women at the tomb, we are filled with terror and amazement. Awe and wonder is the only appropriate response to the good news of resurrection.

The women receive a commission to share the good news with the male disciples. But, do they? As Mark suggests, "they said nothing to anyone because they were afraid." Do they suddenly regain their voice and shout from the mountaintops that Christ is alive? We will never know, but we have heard the message. We have heard the good news of God's everlasting life and the victory of life over death. We have been restored to life because Jesus lives and we can now face tomorrow in all its complexity.

So What? We have heard the Christmas and Easter stories so often that they have lost their element of surprise and spiritual edge. We know that there will be a happy ending – the child is born, the angels sing, and Jesus rises from the grave. The tension is gone. Our own stories are much more complicated and uncertain. Is it possible to trust God's resurrection power? Will life triumph over death? Will we die well and be welcomed into God's loving arms?

We can never tame or even understand the resurrection. Awe, and a degree of fear and trembling, cannot be conjured up. Yet, only an awe-filled world can produce a resurrection. It takes launching out on faith alone, and trusting an open future, expecting more than we can ask or imagine from God and ourselves.

Roads Not Travelled. Tell the story from the women's experience. How did they feel as they walked to the tomb? What was it like to arrive at the tomb and find it empty? What kept them from sharing good news? How did it finally get out?

Another adventurous possibility is to write your own ending to Mark's gospel, taking a slightly different path than the second, amended ended. (Mark 16:9-20) What images of new life emerge from your story? What hope does your gospel give to those who must die, mortals like us?

SPIRITUAL PRACTICES
FOR THE PREACHER AND CONGREGATION

Affirmative Faith. Mark's Easter story involves an empty tomb and an open future. The stone is rolled away, clearing a pathway to the future.

> *I rise with Christ.*
> *In Christ, my future is open and filled with adventure.*
> *God has great adventures planned for me our church.*

A Spiritual Practice for Preachers. Read Mark 16:1-8 in the spirit of *lectio divina*, listening for God's insight in the words of scripture. What words or images speak to you? Where are you finding God's wisdom that can guide you through life's obstacles?

Faith at Home. Read Mark 16:1-8 in the spirit of *lectio divina*, listening for God's insights in the words of scripture. Talk as a family about your respective responses to the scripture. What does the resurrection mean to you? How can we understand it in life-changing ways?

PENTECOST:
THE SEASON OF THE SPIRIT

Mark's Pentecostal spirit is lived out in Jesus' day to day encounters. The Spirit of God energizes Jesus to heal the sick and cast out demons. It bends the rules and drives us out of our comfort zones. God's Spirit is always concrete and contextual for Mark. Though ubiquitous in inspiration and empowerment, we can stifle or enhance the Spirit's movements by the quality of our faith. Our faith opens us to new dimensions of reality and in these new dimensions miracles occur. Still the Spirit does not guarantee a stress-free life; it lures Jesus and ourselves toward the cross and embeds us in the pain of the world.

Rejoice! Wherever you are on life's unfolding adventures, the Spirit gives you everything you need to be faithful to God's good news vision.

The Second Sunday after Pentecost
Mark 3:20-35

He's gone over the edge! Our Jesus might just be crazy! At least that's what some of the locals felt about the up and coming healer and teacher. And, Jesus' family took the local gossip seriously. After all, people are reporting that he's speaking with demons, describing himself as God's beloved child, and even claims to talk with God and that God talks back! He always had mystical side, and he and John certainly were quite a pair, with their studies, prayer vigils, and retreats with the Essenes. But, going out on the road as a Messianic teacher, that's the last straw!

Worried by reports of his behavior and concerned that he might have a fate similar to John the Baptist, Jesus' family prepare to make an intervention. They want to bring him home, talk some sense into him, and put him back to work in the family business. Having an interest in God is alright; but he's become God intoxicated; he really believes that he's in constant touch with the

71

Almighty and that will only lead to trouble. They just want to protect him, and his safety trumps, in their mind, living out his vocation as God's beloved child.

One evening during the legendary summer of love, I met a wild eyed, long haired hippie-type who claimed to be a great spiritual teacher. Bobby looked me straight in the eye and said, "I'm Jesus. I've come again, and this time I'm going to do it right." Raised in a religious setting in which the Second Coming of Jesus was often invoked, I initially took his words with a degree of seriousness, and went home wondering if he was right. Could Jesus be coming again, and could this be the one? If I didn't follow him, was I going to be left out of God's salvation? Later, I heard that Bobby had been committed to a mental institution as a result of a bad LSD trip. Since this time, I've run into a number of other people, claiming special revelations from God, most of which proved to exhibit signs of mental illness. I believe that people can experience the divine, and experience divine revelations, shaped by their own personal situation. Yet, the line between mental illness and mysticism may be thin, and so I listen carefully to the words from God in the voices of lovers, lunatics, and poets, as Shakespeare proclaims.

Jesus is forced to defend himself. He doesn't invoke Jewish theology or even share a message from his Divine Parent. He says, "Look at the fruits. The demonic can't do the works I do. The demonic is out to hurt you. I'm out to heal you. If Satan has any characteristic, it's his consistency. He's consistently bad, and that's not me."

As I read these words, I wonder what led Jesus' family and friends to doubt his sanity. In the first few chapters, Mark's gospel describes Jesus as a teacher, healer, mystic, and exorcist. He spends time in prayer and communicates with God, and claims to speak for God. Perhaps, the possibility that Jesus is unique in his revealing of God's nature was more difficult for those who knew him in the flesh. After all, he was flesh and blood, worked as a carpenter, went to the bathroom, and caught colds. He may have played sports and gone to school with the neighborhood kids, who have now grown up and wonder what changed the boy they once knew.

The truth can be right in front of you and you may not see it. Family sometimes can pigeonhole you, and this is perhaps what Jesus' family did. After all, Mark's Jesus is much more flesh and blood than the other three gospels: there is no Eternal Word made flesh, angelic visitation, virgin birth, or angelic hymn sing; just a real human being totally in synch with God's vision for his life and the world.

Jesus concludes his defense by affirming another kind of family besides blood relationships. In his society, defined by hereditary blood lines, such a statement is outrageous. But, Jesus proclaims that those who hear his voice and follow his way are a new kind of family: the people of the Way and pilgrims in God's realm. And what a family they are: most of them are unlearned, outcasts, sinners, and unclean, and some are even women! Jesus truly creates a rainbow family, including every level of society, class, and personal condition. Everyone belongs, and those who follow Jesus are welcomed into a new vision of reality, with new values and infinite possibilities.

Sin against the Holy Spirit? In the midst of Jesus' affirmation of a new kind of spiritual family, he slips in a phrase that has puzzled scholars and laity for two thousand years. Jesus asserts that every sin can be forgiven except the sin against the Holy Spirit. We best leave defining this sin a bit vague. We don't need any more spiritual witch hunts and denunciations in our time. My own reading of Jesus' statement is that it involves the recognition that despite God's unconditional grace, we have the freedom to turn away from God over and over again. Our freedom can alienate us from God, and keep us out of God's realm experientially, even when it is all around us and beckoning us homeward.

So What? Today's passage challenges us to examine our own spiritual families. Who is on our list of intimates? With whom do we share common cause? Who do we exclude? What would we do if Jesus showed up teaching, healing, and exorcising demons? How would we respond to a spiritual teacher who had no boundaries in his hospitality and relationships? Would we be the "Grand Inquisitor" from the *Brother's Karamazov* prefer order and security to the radical insecurity and adventure of Jesus' pathway?

Roads Not Travelled. Tell the story of Jesus' encounter with his family from his family's perspective. What inspires their desire to take him home? What would have happened to Jesus if they had prevailed? What signs of mental illness did Jesus exhibit? What if a prophet showed up at church? How would we treat her or him?

SPIRITUAL PRACTICES
FOR THE PREACHER AND CONGREGATION

Affirmative Faith. This week's scripture is challenging to preacher and community alike. It might at first glance seem irrelevant to daily life. Still, looking through the lens of scripture, we can see ourselves and our calling in new ways.

> *I commit myself to Jesus' pathway of healing and hospitality.*
> *My family embraces people of all kinds.*
> *I support Jesus' healing ministry in its many forms.*

A Spiritual Practice for Preachers. This week consider Christ's presence in your relationships and daily life. Make a regular commitment to pause a moment, breathe deeply, and look at the world with Christ's eyes. This is especially transformative when we pause and embrace Christ's vision in the workplace, at a church committee meeting, or with family. See them with Christ's spirit, see only Christ in them.

Faith at Home. After a time of stillness and quiet prayer, reflect as a family on what it means to be family. Outside of your family, who is closest to you? Is family always determined by biology? Is our family a mirror image of ourselves or does it include people who radically differ from us? How might we expand our circle of relationships to include healthy encounters with people of different ethnic, economic, and age groups?

Third Sunday after Pentecost
Mark 4:26-34

God's realm is the most unlikely place on earth. It comes to us gently like a growing seed, and fiercely like tongues of fire. Wherever you assume its absence, it shows up, and you are forever changed. Fragile in many ways, God's realm bursts forth. The seeds of divine spiritual transformation are planted generously. Many possibilities emerge, and some grow to fullness. The good work God begins will come to fulfillment, and it will be a harvest of righteousness, despite challenges, failures, and unexpected twists on the path. How God's realm grows in the world is mysterious. It cannot be guaranteed, predicted, or controlled; it simply bursts forth fruitfully in our lives.

From the smallest seeds, great plants emerge, giving shelter and comfort. Small is surely beautiful in God's realm. A mustard seed, a boy with loaves and fishes, an unexpected encounter, can change the world. This is the wisdom of the mustard seed, and the butterfly effect from chaos theory. A butterfly flapping its wings on Cape Cod where I live can alter the weather patterns on a Pacific beach. What small things are you doing that can change the world? What unnoticed acts performed daily can shape the lives of families and children for the best?

That's the mystery of God's realm; it springs up in surprising ways.

The passage closes with contrasting those who hear the parables superficially and those who receive a deeper wisdom. "Jesus explained everything in private to his disciples." Is there an esoteric circle in the Christian community? Many, such as author Dan Brown, have sought to identify secret societies in Christendom? Is there a secret to Christ's healing ministry that is only revealed to a few? The answer to these questions is not clear: but, one thing is for certain, those who go deeper in their faith will receive greater insights and inspirations. Opening the door to greater experiences of divine energy and wisdom can occur when we pray, immerse ourselves in sacred scriptures, meditate, and participate in the sacraments and services of healing. Grace abounds and all are touched by God. Still, the shape and quality of divine presence is often related to our spiritual practices and commitments.

So What? There are no small acts or small beginnings in the pathway of Jesus. Changing one thing in your life or in the congregation can be catalytic. It can awaken experiences and powers that we thought were beyond us. What small thing can you personally do - and your congregation corporately do - to open the doors to divine wisdom and energy?

75

Roads Not Travelled. Focus on how important we are to God and the achievement of God's vision in the world through the lens of butterflies and seeds. God's wise creativity inspires the flapping butterfly wing and growing seed. Their growth and flight shape God's future and have a role in achieving God's vision in the world.

SPIRITUAL PRACTICES
FOR THE PREACHER AND CONGREGATION

Affirmative Faith. In the spirit of the butterfly effect, consider what small changes you can make that will transform your life.

Small actions lead to great results.
God is working in my life to do great things for the world.
I bring beauty to the world one act at a time.

A Spiritual Practice for Pastors. Meditate upon the reality of small beginnings that can lead to great results in your life personally and professionally. Visualize a seed growing into a great plant. What seed are you planting? See yourself tending and watering it. What plant does it become? How does this plant help others become fruitful?

Faith at Home. Gather the family to see several time lapse videos of growing plants and animals. Talk about what helps and hinders their growth. Talk about what helps and hinders the growth of children and adults. Make a commitment to do one thing to promote the growth of each person and the family as a whole.

The Fourth Sunday after Pentecost
Mark 4:35-41

Mark's Jesus can change the weather as well as peoples' hearts and minds. As the waves engulf their boat, Jesus is calmly sleeping. The disciples panic, fearing for their lives, and rouse the teacher and healer, who wakens, stills the storm, and pointedly asks, "Why were you afraid?"

It has been said that courage is fear that has said its prayers. I have experienced more than a little fear on stormy airplane flights. Pitched like a kite in a blustery wind, the plane seems helpless and in danger of catastrophe. I was consoled on one flight when after we'd passed through the storm, the pilot apologized for the bumpy ride and then said, "We had a few potholes on this flight, didn't we?" That placed what I was experiencing in a larger perspective. What I saw as potentially catastrophic, the pilot saw as challenging but not dangerous. Perhaps the same imagery was at work in Jesus' thinking: there is a storm and it is fierce, but if we let go of our fear, we have the resources to creatively respond to it.

Jesus awakens and calms the storm. I see two miracles in this story. The first occurred when the disciples remembered Jesus was in the boat. Like a child waking up disoriented and alone, and feeling panicked, everything in her or his experience changes when the child remembers her or his parent, grandparent, or caregiver is in the next room. There is a residue of fear, but the child now knows that he or she will be alright. When the disciples remembered Jesus was with them, they still experienced the storm's threat, but now it was placed in perspective, as a finite reality embedded in God's infinite wisdom. The healer was with them and they would be alright. Remembering Jesus calmed their spirits before he calmed the storm.

The second miraculous event involved Jesus' stilling the storm. Now, I do not see miracles as supernatural violations of the laws of nature. I see them as events that occur when we are truly in synch with the world and its deepest energies. In the spirit of the rainmakers and today's butterfly effect, Jesus may have been able to tap into the congruence between the human and non-human world. In the intricate ecology of life, we are well aware that human actions shape nature. Global climate change is the most obvious example of the connectedness of humankind and nature. In that moment, could it have been possible for Jesus' spiritual state to shape the non-human world around him?

Mark follows this story with the account of Jesus healing a man possessed by a legion of evil spirits. We experience both inner and outer storms, and when we are connected with God – touching and being touch by God – we can experience healing and wholeness even when the storms are raging. Some storms may never cease.

We can experience peace when we remember that Christ is in the storm with us, assuring us that all will be well and that we can live in God's abundance regardless of life's circumstances.

So What? Life is change, and individually or in a congregation, positive and negative changes can lead to increased feelings of anxiety for congregants and their pastor. Remembering that God is with you – and may be the source of certain changes we find unsettling – in all of life's transitions gives us hope that we will have the resources to respond creativity to all that life brings us.

Roads Not Travelled. Lead the congregation in a guided meditation exercise on the storm at sea. Have them experience the waves, the panic, the realization of God's presence, and Jesus' stilling the storm.

Muse with the congregation about ways we can change the weather. Reflect on Jesus as a weather maker and the impact of our thoughts on the world around us.

SPIRITUAL PRACTICES
FOR THE PREACHER AND CONGREGATION

Affirmative Faith. Responding to the storms of life is a matter of perspective. When we see ourselves in God's care, the storms may buffet us, but we recognize that no storm can separate us from God's loving care.

> *God is with me in every storm of life.*
> *In all of life's challenges, God guides and protects.*
> *I feel God's calm amid life's turmoil.*

A Spiritual Practice for Preachers. In this spiritual practice, take time to be still in God's presence. Read Mark 4:35-41. Visualize yourself being caught in a severe storm. What is the storm like? How do you feel in the midst of the storm? Then imagine that Jesus is with you in the boat. How does it feel to know that Jesus is your companion? What do you want to share with Jesus?

Visualize Jesus calming the storm, and guiding your boat homeward. What things do you now want to share with Jesus? What wisdom does he impart to you? Conclude by giving thanks to God for being with you in the storms of life.

Faith at Home. After a few moments of silence and prayer, read Mark 4:35-41. Talk about what it means to members of the family. Talk about times we feel afraid and how knowing Jesus is with you can give you a sense of courage. Conclude with a prayer for God's presence in challenging life situations.

Fifth Sunday after Pentecost
Mark 5:21-43

Today's readings present a tour de force of Christ's healing ministry. While these passages are not prescriptive, they describe several important pathways of healing. I believe that Jesus' healing ministry represents a heightening of the energy that created the universe and that is resident in our cells and souls. Jesus' healing ministry –and our own – is not contrary to the laws of nature, but an expression of the powers available to us when we are fully in synch with our deepest selves, God, the well-being of others, and our environment. Then and now, Jesus' healing ministry is more than sociological and political, although it includes these factors, but spiritual and physical in the most holistic ways possible.

Mark 5:21-43 contains two healing stories: the healing of Jairus' daughter bookends the account of the healing of the woman with the flow of blood. Jairus is wealthy, the unnamed woman is impoverished. Yet, Jairus, like the woman, is feeling powerless and desperate, and calls upon the only one who can save. His daughter is in a coma and near death. He beseeches the healer Jesus to come to his house, and Jesus leaves immediately to respond to his need. As the father of a cancer survivor, I know how desperate I felt when my daughter-in-law called us with news that our son had been hospitalized. I dropped everything and drove the 120 miles from Lancaster, Pennsylvania, to Washington D.C. I was afraid and initially certain that he was going to die. I would have done anything and would have moved heaven and earth to insure his survival. I would have changed places and taken his pain on myself. Jesus the healer felt Jairus' pain, and nothing would stand between him and restoring this young girl to health.

The path to healing is often surprising. On the way, a woman reaches out to Jesus and is healed. Plagued by what most scholars describe as a gynecological ailment, her illness had alienated her from husband (if she had one) as well as family, community, and religion. She was a social and spiritual outcast and, like many people today, impoverished by the cost of health care. Perhaps she even internalized the social judgments heaped upon her, wondering if somehow she might have committed a sin that led to her ailment or if God was punishing her for some sin of which she was unaware. For her, the healing moment was now! In her desperation, she found the courage to face the crowds, the stares, and comments, and the risk of rejection from the healer. This was her time and she wasn't going to let it pass. It was now or never and she pushed her way toward the healer, guided and sustained by her affirmation, "If I but touch his clothes, I will be made well." I imagine her repeating this over and over, so that it became the lens through which she viewed her future.

When she touches Jesus, the healing energy of the universe is released. A power flows from Jesus that heals her cells as well as her soul. The power is so great that it unsettles the healer, who looks all around for the recipient of his energy. Healed, she comes to him, elated but filled with fear and trembling at what she just experienced and how he might respond to her. She receives his final blessing, "Daughter, your faith has made you well."

Thankfully, this, like so many of Jesus' healings, is many-faceted. Her faith is a factor, but not the only factor in her healing. This passage is misused if we see it fully dependent on her faith. By implication, those who are not healed somehow lack the faith that transformed her life. In truth, her healing came from a divine synchronicity of her faith and divine power. Her faith opened the door to healing power residing in the healer. Healing is not about us, but a synergetic connection of our faith, the faith of others, our condition and previous behavior, the nature of the illness and medical responses, and God's ever-present goal of abundant life.

The healing of Jairus' daughter is also the result of the interplay of faith and divine power. Jesus dismisses the naysayers and allows only those who trust his diagnostic (she is not dead, but asleep) and healing power. Jesus creates a healing circle to bring about her recovery. Healing is always a communal event, grounded in a community of faith that believes on our behalf. In this healing story, the faith of others opens the girl to God's healing touch. When others are unable to believe, our trust in God can be a tipping point from illness to health, opening up new pathways for God's healing power.

So What? These healing stories invite us to become God's healing companions. We have a role in the healing processes of others, first, by eliminating social stigma and ostracism for persons facing serious illness. Second, we can create ministries of healing and wholeness in our congregation and claim our role as God's healing partners. Our faith matters and can make the difference in healing and illness of ourselves and others.

Roads Not Travelled. There are many possible routes from the sermon to the world. Follow the worship service with a healing circle, involving prayer and anointing with oil. Another option is to explore the nature of miracles. What can we believe about "acts of God?" What about supernaturalism? Does God violate the laws of nature or is healing naturalistic in nature, a lively enhancement of the energies residing in all things? Are there any keys to divine healing?

SPIRITUAL PRACTICES
FOR THE PREACHER AND CONGREGATION

Affirmative Faith. Today's readings are chock full of affirmations. In fact, the healing process found in these passages is grounded in affirmative faith and trust that God's resources are greater than our own and can transform our lives.

> *My faith is making me whole.*
> *My faith helps transform peoples' lives.*
> *God's healing energy flows in and through me.*

A Spiritual Practice for Preachers. Take time to imagine that you are this woman. What ailment is standing between you and God's abundant vision for your life and ministry? In what ways has this ailment limited you? After pondering these questions, visualize yourself walking toward Jesus. See the crowd and the teacher walking toward you in the distance. What does Jesus look like? What do you say to yourself as you walk toward him? Do you have an affirmation? If so, repeat as you come closer step by step.

At last, you are next to Jesus. You reach out and experience Jesus' healing power flowing through you. Feel you cells and souls transformed. Jesus now approaches you. What does he say to you? How do you respond to him? Conclude by giving thanks for God's blessing of healing in your life.

Faith at Home. Walter Wink once said that the future belongs to the intercessors. In your family prayer time, talk about what faith means and how it can change your life. Listen to each one's understanding of the role of faith in changing our lives. Conclude with a time of prayer for each member of the family and for persons identified as needing our prayers and love.

Sixth Sunday after Pentecost
Mark 6:1-13

"And he could do no deed of power there, except that he laid his hands on a few sick people and cured them. And he was amazed at their unbelief." Mark is a profoundly dialogical gospel. God is sovereign and powerful, and yet God's power in the world depends on human faith. Our openness or resistance to God's way can help or hinder God's vision in the world. God never gives up on us, but God's presence in our lives and communities is profoundly shaped by our spiritual practices, faith, and openness to transformation.

Jesus' neighbors challenge his ministry and are offended by his so-called "special powers." Their unbelief minimizes the flow of Jesus' healing power, limiting him to a few undramatic healings! This is a stark contrast from the faith of three strangers – the woman with the flow of blood and Jairus and his wife. They trusted that God was at work in Jesus' life and that God's power could transform their lives. When we trust God – opening to the one who stands at the door and knocks – powers are released and, in the spirit of John's Gospel, we can do greater things. (John 14:12) In contrast, when we turn away from God's vision, we put barriers between God's power and ourselves. Healing is always personal and contextual and God's care comes to our particular, and not an abstract or ideal, situation.

The second section of today's reading describes Jesus' commissioning of his disciples to minister two by two, teaching, preaching, and healing. Trusting God, they journey throughout the countryside sharing good news of God's realm and demonstrating it by healing the sick. Their healing involves anointing with oil. Oil is a traditional medium of healing, and is often used in today's healing services. Joined with prayer, anointing can open us to God's presence in our lives and bring comfort and spiritual and physical well-being to those whom we touch in prayer.

So What? This passage once again explores the power of faith to transform our lives. It also invites us to consider the communal nature of healing. Can the faith of communities enhance or hinder God's presence in our lives? Where does our congregation need to focus on the healing of individuals and the community? What difference do our prayers and faith make on the well-being of others? What would happen if we had an experiment in healing prayer as a congregation?

Roads Not Travelled. Invite the congregation to write on pieces of paper, labeled "I need a healing," a condition that requires God's healing touch. Invite them to also write down the name of someone in need of God's healing touch. Place all of these in a basket to be included in the pastoral prayer. Keep these prayer pages for a week, praying every day for God's healing energies to transform those for whom you are praying.

SPIRITUAL PRACTICE
FOR THE PREACHER AND CONGREGATION

Affirmative Faith. Our faith and unfaith can open us to greater or lesser manifestations of God's healing energy. While God is always working in our lives, we can block or enhance the flow of God's energy of love in our lives. Affirmations open the door to divine wholeness in us and others.

> *My faith opens the door to God's energy of love.*
> *I reach out to God and others for healing and wholeness.*
> *I open to God's healing power for myself and others.*

A Spiritual Practice for Preachers. As a spiritual practice, consider the following: What are your thoughts about Jesus' healing ministry and our role as God's healing partners today? What can your congregation do to promote healing and wholeness? Experiment with healing prayer for yourself and others.

Faith at Home. Once more the focus is on faith and prayer. Around your family circle reflect on the prayers that each member lifts up. Take time to join hands and pray together for your family's needs and the needs of others.

The Seventh Sunday after Pentecost
Mark 6:14-29

The beheading of John the Baptist is a revelation of the shadow side of political and spiritual leadership. Herod is ambivalent about John. He dislikes John's message but finds the wild prophet intriguing. He realized that John was his shadow: a holy man living simply and preaching a message of simplicity and monasticism in contrast to Herod's moral depravity, opulence, materialism, and violence. Yet, as the scripture says, Herod liked to hear John speak and took pains to protect him, even from the schemes of his wife Herodias.

Still, Herod's carnality and moral weakness got the better of him. Enchanted by Herodias' daughter's dance, he offers her anything she wants. Behind his power and violence lay a man without inner strength or a moral compass. He could not retract his decision and was forced to have John beheaded. Still, John's death was not solely Herodias' fault. Despite her evil intent, it was Herod who made the decision, and who lacked the strength to change his mind.

So What? This passage challenges us to explore our own character. Are we strong enough to withstand temptation? Do our passions overrule what we know is best for us and others? Do we succumb to moral weakness or can we withstand the powers that threaten to seduce us? I think we can all speak from experience of wanting to do the right thing and then backing down or succumbing to temptation or a lesser good.

It would be a mistake to identify Herod's weakness entirely with sexuality. He is overcome by lust and desire, and our desires can be for wealth, power, food, alcohol, drugs, and sexuality. We can also lust for prominence and acknowledgement in our field, a more comfortable life, security and a good retirement. We can surrender our moral and spiritual compass for temporary benefits and pleasures.

Roads Not Travelled. Tell the story from Herod's point of view. Liberate the ruler from the cardboard prison of scripture to become a living, breathing, ambivalent figure. What were his feelings? How did he feel after her realized what he had set in motion? Did he have regrets? How did his life unfold?

You might also tell the story from the perspective of Herodias and her daughter. Have them share their feelings about the incident. Perhaps, the Herodias' daughter eventually regretted her role in the death of the prophetic messenger.

SPIRITUAL PRACTICES
FOR THE PREACHER AND CONGREGATION

Affirmative Faith. In the challenges of life, the storms at sea and life's temptations, God is with us. God never abandons us though we are often forgetful of God. Affirmations remind us of God's ever-present guidance and strength.

God is with me in times of temptation.
God gives me wisdom and courage to make the right decision.
I follow God's moral compass in my decision-making.

A Spiritual Practice for Preachers. This reading is a tough one, and we are tempted to see no spiritual guidance emerging from it. Yet, it is rich as an examination of conscience. Take some time for stillness, breathing deeply God's healing spirit. After you feel a sense of spiritual centeredness, take a prayer walk, reflecting on your greatest gifts as a pastor and leader. Give thanks for these gifts and ask for God's blessing upon your gifts.

Then, in the course of your walk, reflect on your greatest personal temptations and their impact on your spiritual leadership. Invite God's inspiration and strength to keep you from temptation, and to use your temptations as pathways to blessing. Circle yourself in divine love and light.

Faith at Home. Take time as a family for a time of stillness and quiet prayer. After a few minutes, take time for a conversation on what is most important to you as persons and as a family. Reflect together about what might stand in the way of doing what's most important. Pray for guidance, the ability to make good decisions, and strength in the face of temptation.

Eighth Sunday after Pentecost
Mark 6:30-34, 53-56

Today's readings connect contemplation and healing. Jesus and his disciples are in great demand. Indeed, as Mark interestingly notes, the disciples are so busy that "they had no leisure even to eat!" Multi-tasking in the first century! Certainly many pastors and laypeople seem overwhelmed by their duties, and near burnout and compassion fatigue. As they eat their fast food lunch, they check e-mail, make calls, and text, and allow themselves no time for refreshment and rejuvenation.

Jesus wisely takes his disciples on a retreat. They go to a deserted place and though the crowds anticipate their destination, they have an opportunity to be alone and off-duty. We are tempted to spiritualize their time together. Perhaps, they prayed and entered into deep silence. They may also have told stories, laughed, napped, played, and shared a good meal. They needed refreshment to carry on with their ministry.

Jesus recognizes the reality of human suffering but also knows that our ability to respond creatively and energetically requires that we withdraw for spiritual, emotional, and physical refreshment. We can become so spiritually depleted that we are no earthly good. Our burnout can lead to polarization, cynicism, and alienation from those we are seeking to help.

As they return to shore, the crowds are waiting, and like sheep without a shepherd, seeking guidance, healing, and spiritual nurture. Mark notes that though their presence may have cut short Jesus' retreat, Jesus had compassion on them. Jesus is spiritually and emotionally restored and can now respond to others' spiritual emptiness with an open heart. Meditation, prayer, Sabbath time, play, and companionship are the most effective antidotes to compassion fatigue and stress-induced illness. Mark notes that Jesus sought silence at various times throughout his ministry. Perhaps Jesus had a daily routine of contemplative prayer and reflection on scripture.

The compassionate Jesus teaches, preaches, feeds a multitude, and once again immerses himself in silence. (Mark 6:46) As he continues his journey, he is once more surrounded by people in need. They are so hopeful and desperate that even touching his cloak will suffice to transform their lives. As Mark notes, "All who touched his cloak were healed." Surely these healings were synergetic, like the woman with the flow of blood and Jairus' daughter. Deep human faith met God's desire to heal and unexpected energies were released. These are the energies embedded in our cells and souls, and available to transform us body, mind, spirit, and relationship. The interplay of faith, the placebo effect, and the spiritual centeredness of another, can release "miraculous" energies that cure bodies, restore spirits, and enable us to live gracefully with chronic and incurable conditions.

So What? Today's lectionary highlights action and contemplation. Contemplation can slow down our perception of time and give us a larger perspective. Congregants and pastor alike need to respond to life's challenges from a place of spiritual, emotional, and physical well-being. We need to consider practices that enable us to join spiritual depth with commitment to social justice and interpersonal healing.

Reads Not Travelled. Preach about what happened on Jesus' retreat with his disciples. What did they do together? Was it all business or did they play as well? What would you want to do to restore your spirit if you went on retreat with Jesus?

SPIRITUAL PRACTICES
FOR THE PREACHER AND CONGREGATION

Affirmative Faith. Many pastors are unable to relax. They feel that they must be available and on duty 24/7 to respond to potential crises in the congregation. I recall one pastor confessing that she chose not to drink alcohol because "someone might call me and I want to be ready." While her commitment to 24/7 ministry is laudable, Jesus took another pathway. Occasionally he went off duty, trusting God with the present and future, and recognizing that his spiritual health shaped the quality of his ministry.

I take time each day and throughout the week to open to God's presence.
I take time for adequate rest and refreshment for responding to the needs of others.
Refreshed by God's presence, I have compassion on others.

A Spiritual Practice for Preachers. Consider the following questions: Do you have a "deserted place" for retreat and refreshment? What healthy activities reduce your stress and refresh your spirit? If you struggle two respond to these questions, take time to prayerfully ask God to direct you to a meditative place. Invite God to reveal to you positive ways your can respond to stress.

Today, take time to be still. Open to God's presence through a prayer word such as "joy," "peace," "love," and "God." In the spirit of centering prayer, let this be your search light to illuminate God's presence in your life.

Faith at Home. People of all ages can learn to meditate. I have spent a few moments of stillness with my three year old grandson. We take a few breaths, close our eyes, and then I say a prayer with him.

Take a few times each week with your whole family to do a family meditation. Here is one pattern:

- Begin with a scripture such as "pause awhile and know that I am God."
- Close your eyes and breathe deeply.
- Continue breathing gently, experiencing a sense of calm and peace.
- Close with a prayer of thanksgiving for all the good things in your lives.

The Fourteenth Sunday after Pentecost
Mark 7:1-8, 14-15, 21-23

Jesus is once again in controversy with the religious leaders. Now, we need to remember that the Pharisees were not evil, nor did they lack spirituality. In a time of upheaval, they sought to achieve at least one element of order in peoples' lives. They wanted to maintain their identity as Jewish people in an environment in which their religious identity was at stake. Today, we might compare them to people in our churches who remember the good old days and try to hold onto traditions even when they no longer address 21st century ways of life. They are trying to leave a legacy and insure the survival of the church in the only way they know, by the practices of the 50's and early 60's. The intent is laudable but often stifling to new ways of following Jesus.

Mark's Jesus takes a much less charitable view toward the Pharisees than I do. Remember, he is not referring to all Pharisees, but a particular attitude among the religious leaders toward his spiritual movement. To universalize that all Pharisees were out to get Jesus comes perilously close to anti-Judaism. Jesus accuses them of being righteous on the outside and spiritually bankrupt on the inside. Although this judgment may be too harsh, it is nevertheless a reminder to us: take care of your inner life and relationship with God. External behaviors are meaningful only when they reflect inner integrity. We need to balance the inner and outer life. What we do is still important. We need to be "decent and in order" in the conduct of our worship, governance, and spiritual leadership. But, these practices are valuable only if they are connected with vital, heart-felt, and intimate experience of the divine.

In contrast to Jesus' words about the importance of inner spiritual fire, there is some truth to the statement "Fake it until you make it." The practices of faith are not contingent on how we feel. We may meditate, go to church, preach sermons, and lead bible studies when we seem most alienated from God. We may visit congregants in nursing homes and hospitals on days when our hearts are not in these tasks. The practices of spiritual care and hospitality are life-changing even when our spirits are most withered and dry. Still, our role as people of faith is to see ritual as secondary to experience and religious laws as subservient to experiences of joy and healing.

So What? This passage begs a number of questions: What are the "sacred cows" of your congregation? What persons in your congregation yearn for the way things were at church fifty years ago? Are their intentions always negative? What positive values motivate them? In what ways can we nurture inner experiences of God so that our rituals are vital and life-giving?

Roads Not Travelled. Tell the story from the point of view of one of the Pharisees. What values are important to them? Why is Jesus such a threat? What bothered them about Jesus' spiritual flexibility?

SPIRITUAL PRACTICES
FOR THE PREACHER AND CONGREGATION

Affirmative Faith. The following affirmative prayers can help you keep your faith alive and flexible in challenging times.

> *I am open to new possibilities of faithfulness to God.*
> *My inner life is vital and lively.*
> *I join order and novelty in my spiritual life and leadership.*

A Spiritual Practice for Preachers. In this week's spiritual practice, explore doing an old thing in a new way both in your spiritual life and congregational leadership. What new practice might you embody to give greater energy and life to your ministry? As you ponder new possibilities for life and ministry, take a fifteen minute walk through your home or congregation environment. What new things do you notice? As your body moves, new ideas may emerge.

Faith at Home. After a time of prayer, consider as a family what family rituals are most life-giving and essential? What family rituals are unnecessary and unhelpful, given your current family situation? What alternative practices might you explore as a family to reach the right balance of order and novelty?

The Fifteenth Sunday after Pentecost
Mark 7:24-37

The story of Jesus' encounter with a Syrophoenician woman is one most curious accounts of Jesus' ministry. My first reaction as a preacher is "why did Mark include this story if his goal was to portray Jesus' uniqueness as God's beloved son and messenger to humankind?" It doesn't put Jesus in a very good light. He appears to embody all of the following unflattering traits: racism, sexism, impoliteness, grumpiness. He doesn't even appear to want to heal this young girl, despite the mother's pleas. He appears simply to want to eat his meal in peace, undisturbed by the local riff-raff.

I have three interpretations of Jesus' attitude toward this vulnerable foreigner. The first, most literal interpretation: Jesus has not yet discerned that his mission is global and he is, frankly, exhibiting the racist attitudes many Jews had toward Gentiles, especially those who had been their neighbors for centuries. The woman's persistence softens Jesus' heart and changes his mind. She teaches him that his mission goes far beyond Israel. A second interpretation suggests that Jesus was testing her. His actions were a spiritual challenge: "How badly do you want your daughter to be healed? Are you willing to sacrifice everything for her healing?" Obviously the woman passed the test. Like many parents of seriously ill children, she is willing to sacrifice her pride and, perhaps, a lot more for her child to be cured. A third interpretation asserts

91

that Jesus is taking part in a theological "bait and switch," unknown initially to his Jewish companions. Jesus is invoking quite callously the racist and sexist attitudes they may all have shared and then, after everyone nods their head in agreement that this woman is no more than a Gentile dog, deserving absolutely nothing, he goes ahead and cures her daughter, pulling out the rug from all of them. The encounter is a type of parable in which we expect one outcome and then get another.

In any case, the woman persists, matching wits with Jesus, and her daughter is healed at a distance. Recently, scientists have been studying the power of distant intentionality or intercessory prayer. While the results are not fully conclusive, the research suggests an association between prayer at a distance and better health outcomes. Joined with the butterfly effect, this research suggests that we are intimately connected and that our prayers and visualizations, our thoughts and feelings, radiate across the universe, creating a healing field of force in the lives of those for whom we pray. Anecdotal evidence suggests that there is no geographical or physical distance in prayer and that when we pray for another person, we truly are right beside them in spirit, bringing positive energies into their lives.

The second healing story focuses on a man with hearing and speech impairments. In this story, Jesus employs a type of healing ritual: he looks heavenward, touching the man's ears and placing spittle on his tongue. We don't know if Jesus used any ritualistic techniques in his healing ministry. He healed people using a variety of methodologies, inviting us to do likewise, and use those healing practices that work best for us and in our communities.

Mark is the healing gospel. Jesus' power and authority as God's beloved child is revealed in transformed lives, in the healing of body, mind, spirit, and relationships. In the spirit of the last of the written canonical gospels, Mark invites us to be part of Jesus' healing ministry, embodying greater things (John 14:12) in our spiritual leadership and congregational lives.

So What? This passage invites us to go in a variety of homiletical directions. We can approach the text as a challenge to racist and sexist attitudes. The unflattering portrait of Jesus invites us to examine our own "isms" and find ways to go beyond them to respond to human need. The passage also challenges us to reflect on our attitudes toward prayer. Do we pray for others? Do we believe prayer makes a difference in their lives? What would happen if we made a commitment as a congregation to be a laboratory for prayer?

Roads Not Travelled. Imagine a sermon entitled "Jesus the Racist" as a window into reflecting on our own "ism's." You might also tell the story from the point of view of the Syrophoenician woman. How did she respond to Jesus' apparent racism? What kept her going in spite of his negative response? How did she feel when she returned home? You might also follow third interpretation and explore the story from the point of view of one of the self-satisfied onlookers who suddenly finds his world turned upside down.

SPIRITUAL PRACTICES
FOR THE PREACHER AND CONGREGATION

Affirmative Faith. This passage invites us to be bold in prayer and hospitality. Our spiritual affirmations can change our hearts and minds.

> *I pray boldly for God's healing touch.*
> *I welcome strangers and persons of different ethnicities as God's beloved children.*
> *I push the boundaries of my comfort zone to follow God's way.*

A Spiritual Practice for Preachers. Let your own life be a laboratory for joining hospitality and prayer. Take time regularly to pray for the needs of others, soaking them in God's blessings, and asking for healing and transformation. Pray especially for persons of other ethnic groups and sexual orientations, recognizing that prayer joins you in common cause as God's beloved children.

Faith at Home. After a few moments of stillness, open with a brief prayer. Talk about people who are in need of our prayers and the difference prayer might make in their lives and our own. Write their names on pieces of paper and pass them out to each family member. Make a commitment to pray at least once a day each person or situation.

Sixteenth Sunday after Pentecost
Mark 8:27-38

Today's scripture invites us to meet Jesus again – for the first time. Long before Marcus Borg's insightful book, many people perceived Jesus as a mystery, almost inscrutable. No doubt they projected their positive and negative images upon him – Messiah who would overthrow Roman occupation, the return of Elijah or Moses, the one who will usher in the New Jerusalem, a heretic, a phony, a threat to our faith and nation.

Jesus wants to assess where his disciples stand on his identity. He begins indirectly, "Who do people say that I am?" Then, he asks the key question for the disciples and us, "Who do you say that I am?" Our answer to this question will determine our values, spiritual practices, and understanding of the world. Jesus is always personal, never abstract. He is flesh and blood, and asks us to follow him in our flesh and blood lives.

Dan Brown's *Da Vinci Code* caused a great deal of controversy with the suggestion that Jesus' relationship with Mary of Magdala might have been marital as well as spiritual and that from their love from each other, a child was born. Years prior Brown's book, the movie *Last Temptation of Christ* adapted from Nikos Kazantzakis' book, created a furor among evangelical and fundamentalist Christians – and demonstrations at movie theatres – because its depiction of Jesus' mystical experiences and its suggestion that Jesus could have bypassed the cross and chosen a quiet domestic life with Mary of Magdala. While we don't know the character of Jesus' intimate relationships, the furor over the film suggested that certain Christians could not tolerate the possibility that Jesus might have enjoyed sexual relations. This said more about them and their view of sexuality than it did about our Savior. Their objections implied that somehow sexuality is dirty and unworthy of God. From their point of view, our Savior always thought of ethereal, heavenly, and non-physical things, and that sexuality can never be an avenue to experiencing the holy.

94

Mark's Jesus is very earthy. He touches bodies, heals with spit, enjoys good meals, gets cranky (or appears to be grumpy), needs a regular prayer life, and requires rest. Jesus' ministry is aimed at whole people, not disembodied spirits. This is the point of the dialogue about Jesus' identity. Peter gets it, "You are the Christ, the Son of the Living God." But, when Jesus suggests that the he might suffer, Peter rebukes him. His rebuke is both personal and theological. He can't imagine his teacher suffering. He also can't imagine God's chosen one experiencing pain and death directly.

Jesus' Messianic identity defies our understanding of power and relationships. God's power is not unilateral or coercive, but in the spirit of Philippians 2:5-11, is relational, intimate, and dialogical. God's beloved one suffers and God does, too! Only a suffering God can save, asserted Dietrich Bonhoeffer. God is the fellow sufferer who understands, affirmed Alfred North Whitehead. "God is with us" is an empty phrase apart from the recognition that God's presence means sharing in our joy and sorrow. What we do and feel matters to God, shapes God's experience, and adds to or subtracts from God's ability to transform the world.

The Messiah is our model. Those who grasp onto their lives will lose them. Those who sacrifice self-made, isolated individualism will save their lives. One of my teachers Bernard Loomer spoke of "size" or "stature" as a primary religious virtue. Stature involves the scope of our embrace of the world. It involves how much reality we can experience whole-heartedly without losing our spiritual center. Jesus' statements invite us to grow in spirit and stature and to see our well-being and the well-being of others as interconnected: their joy is our joy and their pain is our pain.

So What? What are we holding onto for dear life as persons and as a congregation? What would happen if we let go and trusted God? Would it make any difference to know that God is in the mix with us, feeling our joy and pain, and rooting us on toward wholeness and mission?

Roads Not Travelled. An adventurous preacher might focus on "dying God, dying church" and consider what's worth dying for personally and institutionally. Another might be, "When dying is good for your health."

SPIRITUAL PRACTICES
FOR THE PREACHER AND CONGREGATION

Affirmative Faith. Affirmations open us to a wider world and take us beyond self-interest to care for the world.

> *I am growing in wisdom and stature.*
> *I let go of limits and open to God's abundant possibilities.*
> *God is with me in joy and sorrow.*

A Spiritual Practice for Preachers. After a generous silence, take time to explore your images of Jesus. Under what guises does Jesus come to you? What characteristics of Jesus are most exemplary to you? What does this mean for your own spiritual practice?

Faith at Home. Go on line and find a variety of pictures, both classical and contemporary. Talk about what they mean and what you think Jesus might look like. What characteristics of Jesus most attract you? Which of these can you embody on a daily basis?

See:

http://www.divinerevelations.info/documents/jesus_pictures/jesus_christ_pictures.htm;

http://www.goodsalt.com/search/jesus.html)

Seventeenth Sunday after Pentecost
Mark 9:30-37

The disciples don't seem to get it, and neither do we. After all this time, the disciples still struggle to understand Jesus' mission. They can't imagine the possibility that the way of salvation passes through Jerusalem and the cross. Nor can they fully grasp that in Jesus' realm, where power is relational and sacrificial rather than authoritarian and coercive. Despite Jesus' message of sacrificial love, the disciples argue about who will be the greatest in God's realm. They focus on the solitary ego and its place in the world rather than the interdependent realm of God, in which all of our souls expand to embrace the whole earth and beyond.

Jesus challenges our hierarchical thinking by asserting that the greatest must be a servant, who places the needs of others above her or his own. Spiritual leadership is immersed in the rough and tumble challenges of life, right here in the messiness of everyday life. Spiritual greatness involves largeness of soul in which our well-being and the well-being of others are interrelated, and put on equal footing.

Jesus places the child at the heart of God's realm. Those who care for God's children, especially those who are the most vulnerable and from whom you receive no reward, are near the heart of God. The beloved community embodied in Jesus' radical hospitality and table fellowship embraces all humankind, but has a preferential concern for the most vulnerable members of our communities, which includes children who were expendable in the first century and victims of neglect, unsafe working conditions, and human trafficking in our own time.

Mark's words have a special kinship to "mind of Christ," described in Philippians 2:5-11. Having the mind of Christ involves celebrating interdependence. It is not above others, but with others. Like the Tao, it works within the concreteness of life, persistent, empowering, and leading by a vision. As communities of faith, our calling is to celebrate Christ's mind as the ideal for spiritual interdependence and personal stature.

So What? What would happen if we saw others' well-being as important as our own? For some of us, we experience this largeness of soul in relationship to our spouses and children. Jesus calls us to define greatness in ways that defy our current social values. Greatness is not about celebrity status, wealth, winning, or political power, but service to others. It may be about downward mobility rather than upward mobility, and about living simply in our consumerist society so others can simply live.

Roads Not Travelled. What sermon titles might emerge from the text this week? "Death to the Ego," "A Leader who Really Served," "The Tao of Christian Leadership," emerge and then might be redacted by identifying and challenging the Caesars in church and the world.

SPIRITUAL PRACTICES
FOR THE PREACHER AND CONGREGATION

Affirmative Faith. Affirmations help us explore new personal and social values. They help us see the world through the eyes of Christ.

> *My well-being is connected with the well-being of others.*
> *I am guided by the mind of Christ.*
> *I let go of possessiveness and open to world consciousness.*

A Spiritual Practice for Preachers. As an examination of conscience, consider your understanding of greatness in ministry. How does it shape your relationships in the church? How does it influence your decisions as congregational leader and your approach to diversity in your congregation? What changes in attitude and action are you willing to make to be more attuned to the mind of Christ?

Faith at Home. Explore ways as a family that you can serve one another. What can you do to bring greater joy to one another? What one sacrifice can you make to support the well-being of others, including persons outside your family?

Eighteenth Sunday after Pentecost
Mark 9:38-50

How do we best deal with religious pluralism? Do we deny it, condemn it, embrace it without investigation, or filter it through the lenses of faith?

While creeds still have value as guideposts of faith, most congregations no longer see them as litmus tests of orthodoxy or boundaries between the saved and unsaved. In fact, many of our most conservative congregants would be hard pressed to identify the Nicene or Apostles Creeds, not to mention the Westminster or Heidelberg confessions. They might invoke more modern criteria of faith such as biblical inerrancy, the virgin birth, the Lordship of Christ, the Second Coming, substitutionary atonement, as the heart of faith. Still, other Christians – I suspect the majority – are essentially non-creedal, focusing on our relationship with God, the value of community, social justice, and religious experience as central to the Christian life. Non-creedal approaches, in spite of their theological minimalism, may be beneficial in a pluralistic age, since creeds have more often than not served as tools of exclusion and condemnation than affirmation and welcome. It is hard to wage a holy war if your doctrinal understandings are theologically fluid and somewhat nebulous.

In today's passage, once again, the disciples don't get it. They return to Jesus, patting themselves on the back and expecting his approval, when they report their silencing of a heretic. Another healer, who is not part of their community, is providing healing to persons struggling with demon possession. In their minds, even if he is easing pain, his work is suspect because he has not gone through the "approved" channels, that is, through their particular community of Jesus' followers.

Jesus challenges their narrow theology, asserting that if someone is doing healing work, he or she is one of us, even if he or she comes from a different community or interpretation of faith. What is important is the healer's care for others: her or his willingness to relieve pain and restore people to wholeness. God's realm embraces diversity and welcomes all who seek to be God's companions in healing the world.

Jesus advises his followers to prune away – to cut off – everything that separates them from God. Jesus is not clear what, in particular, keeps us from knowing God. But, some deterrents to God-awareness are inhospitality, exclusion, and doctrinal correctness. God comes to us in many guises. In focusing on the authorized approaches to God, which of course are really relative to a particular community, we may miss God's many pathways to healing and exclude potential healing partners.

So What? Today's reading challenges us to go beyond in-group, out-group thinking, whether it is motivated by liberalism or conservatism. We cannot limit God's vehicles for revelation and healing. Divine healing comes through anointing and laying of hands, but also medication, surgery, traditional Chinese medicine, visualization exercises, yoga, reiki, and acupuncture.

Roads Not Travelled. The adventurous preacher might use this week's reading as an opportunity to explore non-Western approaches to healing and their relationship with Christian faith. He or she could build bridges with reiki healing touch, acupuncture, tai chi, qigong, Ayurvedic medicine, and other global healing practices. He or she might also explore the issue of pluralistic visions of truth, and ways to creatively respond to a world in which there are many right answers to most important questions.

SPIRITUAL PRACTICES
FOR THE PREACHER AND CONGREGATION

Affirmative Faith. This many-faceted reading joins our affirmation of pluralism with pruning everything that gets in the way of our spiritual growth and mission as Christ's followers.

I am open to a variety of healing paths.
I look for God's healing touch everywhere.
I let go of everything that stands between me and God.

A Spiritual Practice for Preachers. Explore a non-traditional healing path, either through study or first-hand experience. Open to ways that you can integrate this healing path with your understanding of Christian faith.

Faith at Home. Consider ways that your family can become more healthy through diet, exercise, spiritual practices, or holistic approaches to health and healing. Explore practices that you can do as a family to promote health and well-being.

Nineteenth Sunday after Pentecost
Mark 10:2-16

What are we to do with this passage in the 21st century? It has been used to bludgeon abused spouses and gay and lesbian persons. It has been an instrument of ostracism, violence, and intolerance, rather than an affirmation of healthy marital and family relationships. This, of course, is the problem of seeing scripture primarily as a legal document rather than an expression of the evolving divine-human call and response. When seen legalistically, scripture becomes a vehicle of punishment and exclusion. When seen primarily experientially, scripture becomes a book of affirmations and spiritual practices intended to cultivate intimacy with God in our particular context. Ironically, many persons who use this passage to deny equal rights and justice to gay and lesbians are persons who have been divorced, and at least according to this passage worthy of the same condemnation they mete out to others.

What good is a literalistic preaching on this passage, if half of your congregational has been divorced, and you as preacher have also been divorced and remarried, making you an "adulterer" according to the text? We can't turn back the clock, nor can we stigmatize persons who have divorced. For good or ill, divorce has become routine and "no fault." More challenging is the reality that many women now have children out of wedlock, often adding another generation to the cycle of poverty.

This passage connects the realities and impact of divorce and parental relationships with our affirmation of children. In a world in which children were seen as property, Jesus places children and adults on the same level in terms of personal and social value. The community of faith's vocation is to bless its children, and not only its own children but all the children of the world. In a world in which childhood innocence is undermined through poverty, child labor, and sex trafficking, on the one hand, and media violence and sexuality, consumerism, and parental expectations, on the other, the church needs to be countercultural in providing a safe, slow-paced, relational, and intergenerational environment. The church also needs to seek the elimination of crimes against children, age inappropriate media, and governmental policies that indirectly increase family poverty. Our calling is to follow Jesus and bless the children. When Jesus took the children on his knee, his blessing had a healing impact on them: he restored them to God's image, infused them with healthy divine energy, and welcomed them into God's realm, and so should we!

So What? There is no need to single out divorced persons in interpreting today's scriptures. There is a need to promote positive relationships among spouses and partners, care for our children and the children of the church, and awareness of crimes against children. We need to explore how we as church can end violence and abuse of children, whether physically, emotionally, psychologically, or economically.

Roads Not Travelled. How about a sermon titles and themes such as: "Are You an Adulterer?", "I Wish This Wasn't in the Bible!", "Oh, You Sinners!", "God Hates Divorce?" One could also talk about taking relationships seriously in a crash course on Christian marriage.

SPIRITUAL PRACTICES
FOR THE PREACHER AND CONGREGATION

Affirmative Faith. A relational god calls us to healthy and life-supportive relationships. Healthy relationships are a matter of intentionality and commitment; of placing the well-being of relationships at the heart of our personal and economic values.

> *I express my love for my family in healthy and tangible ways.*
> *I balance my commitment to ministry with my care for my loved ones.*
> *My family life and close relationships are holy ground.*

A Spiritual Practice for Preachers. This week the preacher is invited to explore her or his own relationships with family and other intimates through a serious of questions. After a time of quiet prayer, consider the following: 1) the emotional and quantitative (time) balance between your professional ministry and family life and intimate relationships, 2) the current quality of your close relationships, 3) areas in which growth is needed, and 4) areas which are healthy and strong. Ask for God's guidance to deepen and grow your relationships in healthy ways. Ask for God's wisdom and insight to enable you to stay on a healthy pathway relationally.

Faith at Home. Family life can be a place of blessing. This may not be easy, but after a time of prayerful silence, take time to share what each person appreciates or honors in the others. Take time to give thanks for the uniqueness of each family member. Make a commitment to look for the best in one another. Conclude with a blessing: as each person's name is mentioned, let the others bless her or him in prayer. As your name is mentioned and you are the focus of prayer and blessing, accept the positive energy and good will of your family.

Twentieth Sunday after Pentecost
Mark 10-17-31

Today's readings are scandalous in many ways. They challenge us to explore the nature of "goodness" – divine and human – and the evils of wealth. Challenging wealth in the USA is surely un-American. Virtually everyone aspires for the American way of life and, at the very least, this means a nice home, good automobiles, technological gadgets, savings for college, and a generous retirement plan. Commercials ask us, "how long do I have?" equating the size of our retirement plan with our personal longevity and quality of life. "Will we outlive our money?" they ask. Many of us fall into the middle to upper middleclass category of the "anxious affluent" in contrast to much of the world, whose wealth doesn't extend past tomorrow. We may not be wealthy but we have enough. In fact, we have too much and may have to thin things out for the church's – or our own – yearly garage sale.

Jesus is not necessarily picking on us. Still, we need to get the message. We can be possessed by our possessions and imprisoned by the technologies that are intended to make life easier.

What about the wealthy? The gap between wealth and poverty in the USA is growing, and it is even more pronounced in developing countries. People are losing ground financially and some losing homes and going hungry in the USA while others live in opulence and rig the governmental process to have fewer limits on what they can earn. Many of these people see no conflict between unrestrained capitalism and consumerism and the gospel mandates. Like the wealthy young man who sought Jesus' counsel, they believe they are doing the right things in relationship with individual needs. They may even be generous to charities. But, their wealth is getting in the way of their relationship with God. They are unaware of the relationship of their wealth to others' poverty, the impact of their consumption on the ecosystem, and the human cost of their affluence on families and children. They see Christian ethics primarily as face-to-face and forget the social aspects of our faith, the heart of the prophetic message, relate to corporate behaviors, tax policy and gun violence, adequate schools and health care, and the disparity of wealth and poverty.

Can the wealthy be saved? This is truly "class theology" that would incur the ire of political commentators like Glenn Beck who advised his viewers to leave any church that uses the term "social gospel." The problem with wealth is that it often insulates and isolates, creating a wall between the wealthy and poor. It prevents us from hearing the cries of the poor, and perhaps, as a result of our sense of entitlement and self-sufficiency, our own inner cries for authentic spirituality. In the words of the prophetic tradition, as a result of their neglect of the poor, their inability to experience their pain, the wealthy will experience a famine in hearing the word of God. (Amos 8:11)

This passage contains another curious comment. When the wealthy man describes Jesus as "good teacher," Jesus deflects his praise with "Why do you call me good. No one is good but God alone." Mark's Jesus speaks for God, and also assumes that whatever power and energy he has comes from God's presence in his life. Yet, Mark's Jesus may not have intended to create a religion focusing on him, but rather a spiritual movement focusing on his pathway to God. Jesus was, as John's Gospel asserts, the way shower, reflecting and revealing God's character and showing us how to become God's own beloved children. Jesus exemplifies Iranaeus' affirmation that the glory of God is a person fully alive. Being fully alive means being fully congruent with God's vision and living moment by moment guided by divine wisdom. Jesus is the incarnation of God's realm in our lives, showing us how to live on earth inspired and guided by the values and experience of heaven.

There are no guarantees for those who follow Jesus, but there are great blessings. We can embrace persecution because we share in God's eternal life now and in the future.

So What? It is harder for a rich person to get to God's realm than a camel go through the eye of a needle! Most of our congregants, including the preacher and the writer, are among the world's rich. Our economic anxieties emerge from the fact that we have plenty and are worried that we may have less in the future. What is our wealth preventing us from experiencing? What stands between us and God? In certain circles, opposing same gender marriage is considered unbiblical and demonic. Yet, the bible has just a few rather ambiguous verses on homosexuality and hundreds of passages on the dangers of consumerism, exploitation of the poor, and the gap between the wealthy and the poor. In a Christian nation, we are still content with laws that favor the wealthy and punish the poor. Although Jesus was not a politician, his message and way of life was grounded in the prophetic political tradition. We must ask: "What would Jesus say about the poor? How would Jesus respond to the gap between the wealthy and the poor, both in the USA and across the globe?"

Roads Not Travelled. How about sermon titles and discussions inspired by: "Can the wealthy be saved?" or "Is there hope for the wealthy?" or "Wealth is hazardous to your health?" The adventurous preacher might focus on the scandal of omitting economic passages in scripture while condemning homosexuality and necessary abortions on virtually no biblical evidence.

105

SPIRITUAL PRACTICES
FOR THE PREACHER AND CONGREGATION

Affirmative Faith. Following Jesus' pathway calls for us to embrace transformed values and a new way of life. Affirmations can help us make the right decisions regarding wealth and poverty in our personal and political lives.

> *I place God's realm first in my life.*
> *I live simply so others might simply live.*
> *I trust God with my future, and follow God wherever the*
> *road takes me.*

A Spiritual Practice for Preachers. In this week's spiritual practice, open your senses to poverty in your community. Take time to read your local paper prayerfully. Take a walk around your community, noting the pockets of poverty that surround you. Experience the challenges people face who receive only the minimum wage worker. Experience much maligned homeless persons, persons using social services, and troubled veterans with the eyes of Christ, seeing the holiness within them.

Faith at Home. Read the newspaper together as a family, noting who seems to be forgotten, most vulnerable, and without resources. Take some time to see what activities your church is doing to respond to vulnerable persons. Explore the organizations that respond to families and children. What things can your family do to bring greater joy and well-being to marginalized and vulnerable families and children?

Twenty-first Sunday after Pentecost
Mark 10:35-45

Once again, the disciples don't get it, and neither do we. We vie for place and power, and want to get ahead even if others must suffer for us to achieve successes. We want to be first in line even in the religious life. Even though God promises blessings beyond our imagination, we – like the sons of Zebedee – want God to give us what we want and on our terms without regard to our relationships with others.

Recently, I watched a televangelist make a pitch for contributions. He told his viewers that they can claim their great harvest, all the success that God has planned from them. All they need to do is plant a seed, preferably by Visa, MasterCard, or American Express. In contrast, Jesus asserts that God wants us to have abundant life, and that means for the whole community and not just ourselves. The problem with the prosperity gospel is its guarantee of individualistic success. It's all about us and our well-being. Our greater wealth has no connection with the poverty of others or the well-being of the ecosystem. It sees following God as a type of barter system: you give to God and God will give to you, blessing you without regard to the needs of others. Mission and sacrifice are seldom affirmed as central to the Christian way in the messages of the prosperity preachers.

Jesus believed in another kind of prosperity, a sense of well-being in which we all can share. Jesus' vision of prosperity is about "us" and not "me," about God's people and the good earth and not individual success. The realm of god is about service and sacrifice, and a power and greatness that is unimaginable to those for whom winning is the only thing. In God's realm, we don't' jockey for control, but seek to support others. God's realm is one of interdependence in which giving and receiving are intimately related and there is no place for rugged individualism. The greatest is the servant of others.

So What? If we place service and mission as our goal, then everyone, including ourselves, will have what he or she needs to live fully and abundantly. The health of the individual and community are interconnected. Healthy leaders serve rather than dominate, whether in church, business, or government. Jesus redefined family to include, first, the followers of the way and then the whole earth. Most of us are willing to sacrifice for our children or grandchildren. Jesus invites us to expand the notion of family to include persons in our church and beyond. Our well-being and the well-being of others is so intimately connected that we are willing to sacrifice for goals larger than our own.

Roads Not Travelled. An adventurous preacher might speak about the dangers of self-made individualism or thinking that our success is primarily the result of our own efforts. While agency and initiative are essential to success, they are part of a larger matrix of causes, reflecting the interdependent nature of life.

SPIRITUAL PRACTICES
FOR THE PREACHER AND CONGREGATION

Affirmative Faith. This week's reading challenges us to go beyond self-interest to care for the whole. This involves experience the profound interdependence of life.

> *I am connected with all creation.*
> *I let go of narrow self-interest to care for others.*
> *My spirit is spacious and welcoming.*

A Spiritual Practice for Preachers. As a form of self-examination, consider your own leadership style. Do you affirm otherness? Do you listen to other viewpoints? Do you empower others to fulfill their own gifts? Do you see your work primarily as service and mission rather than personal privilege and success? Take time to ask God for guidance so that you might truly be a spirit-led, faithful, and empowering leader.

Faith at Home. Charles Sheldon's *In His Steps,* a classic of the social gospel movement, asks us to consider the question "What would Jesus do?" in every situation? Concretize this question by reflecting on ways that each member of your family can care for and serve other family members. What things can each of us do to make the others' lives more full? Begin to think about simple ways to serve people beyond your family in daily life.

Twenty Second Sunday after Pentecost
Mark 10:46-52

"What do you want me to do for you?" Jesus asks Bartimaeus. The answer might be obvious, "I want to see," but Jesus' question opens Bartimaeus and ourselves to explore what we really need in life.

More than that, the question reveals the importance of listening in pastoral care. When Jesus asks the question, he affirms Bartimaeus' freedom to respond and guide the healer's work. Jesus does not determine in advance what Bartimaeus needs; he allows Bartimaeus to set the agenda for Jesus' healing ministry. The healing process includes the maximization of freedom and creativity, and helping people voice their own visions. The healer lets go of control so Bartimaeus can experience healing of spirit as well as body. Jesus lets Bartimaeus set the agenda and in so doing invites this sight-impaired man to claim his own personal agency, something that may have been limited by his physical condition.

If you really want to change your life, you have to want it really bad and Bartimaeus wants it real bad. He shouts out for a healing, disturbing the peace with his personal needs. His persistence, like that of the woman with the flow of blood and the Syrophoenician woman, leads to a healing.

"Have mercy upon me." We need mercy, don't we? As proficient as we are in ministry, our only hope is to seek God's mercy. We can't always do it on our own. Our wisdom, understanding, and love are often insufficient. Some Sunday mornings we may not even want to go to work, even though the congregation believes us to be the "main attraction." When we cry out for God's mercy, we remember that we are part of a larger pastoral process. We let God's energy fill us and make us whole personally and professionally. We can't make it on our own in ministry: we need the support of friends and colleagues and the grace of God one moment and one decision at a time.

Jesus' final comment to Bartimaeus is "your faith has made you whole." Once again, this is not an individualistic faith healing. Bartimaeus' faith gets the attention of Jesus and opens both himself and Jesus to a greater influx of divine power. Faith alone cannot transform our lives. Faith uniting our spirits with God's Spirit can bring new energies, possibilities, and wisdom that lead to transformation of body, mind, and spirit. Alone we are lost. In synergy with God's energy and the faith of a healing community, we experience healing, even when a cure is not possible. The divine-human call and response – God's calling and our response; our calling and God's response – can move mountains and give us new sight and insight. Thanks be to God!

So What? Today's readings join persistence, faith, and freedom. The passage from Mark provides the opportunity for the congregants and the church as a whole to ponder - individually and corporately - our deepest desires and respond to God's question to us, "What do you want me to do for you, personally and as a community of faith?"

Roads Less Travelled. The pastor might invite pre-selected people in the congregation to shout out at different times of the sermon, "God, help me! Have mercy!" He or she might explore the meaning of the cry "God have mercy" for 21st century, anxiously affluent congregants.

SPIRITUAL PRACTICES
FOR THE PREACHER AND CONGREGATION

Affirmative Faith. This week's readings challenge us to open to God's mercy and be diligent about our faith. God is ready to respond. What need shall we call out?

> *I have life-transforming faith.*
> *I need God's mercy to be healed.*
> *I bring my pain and joy to God in prayer.*

A Spiritual Practice for Preachers. In this week's practice, visualize yourself in conversation with Jesus. The healer asks you, "What do you want me to do for you?" Take some time to imagine a conversation with Jesus in which you respond to his question. "What do you really want? What is the deepest desire of your heart?" Visualize Jesus moving within your life to bring about abundance for yourself, your loved ones, your congregation, and the world.

Faith at Home. As a family, after a time of stillness and prayer, reflect on your deepest needs, considering the distinction between needs and wants. After noting what you most deeply need, take time to pray to together, and make a commitment to support each other in fulfilling your deepest needs personally and as a family.

Twenty-Third Sunday after Pentecost
Mark 12:38-44

Sixth century spiritual teacher Dorotheos of Gaza described the relationship of humankind and God as being like the relationship of points on the radius of a circle and the center of the circle. Dorotheos invited us to imagine the points moving from the radius to the center of the circle. As they move toward God, the many points of the circle move closer to one another. As they move toward each other, the many points of the circle move closer to God. Loving God does not separate us from one another. Immersing ourselves in loving the world brings us closer to God. We love the creator by loving the creatures. We rightly relate to one another by seeing each other in relationship with God.

This appears to be the crux of Jesus' response to another religious leader, who asks "What is the greatest commandment?" Jesus' answer reflects the best of Jewish spirituality and ethics, "God is One, and love God with your all your heart, and with all your soul, and with all your mind, and with all your strength." This is truly holistic spirituality. We love God with our whole selves, body, mind, spirit, and relationships. Everything we do has a Godward orientation. All things are in God, and God is in all things. Nothing is secular or God-forsaken, all persons and encounters can be windows into the divine.

What might be radical today, given Christianity's undeserved reputation as anti-intellectual and anti-science, is to reflect on loving God with your whole mind. There are Christians who see faith and reason as antithetical, who hold onto to an earth-centered world view, and assert a young earth, six day creation. To such Christians, if faith and science conflict, science is by definition wrong. This has led to the emergence of the new atheists who brand Christianity as intolerant and intellectually weak. Yet, these new atheists' visions of God often go no further than what they learned in early childhood church school. They attack versions of Christianity that most of our congregants would repudiate as well.

Neither Jesus nor the Hebraic tradition he affirmed would have scorned science. They lived in a very different age, with a different cosmology and explanation of the natural world, but they were open rather than closed to the wisdom of the world. Today,

111

we can affirm the findings of science and medicine and integrate them into our understanding of reality and God's work in the world. The problem with biblical literalism and scientism is that both take themselves too seriously, they shrink the world to the pages of a sacred text or to the evidence supplied by the five senses. The world is far too mysterious and complex to be described by ancient creation stories or circumscribed by our current scientific and medical knowledge.

Loving God with your mind means listening to scientists and physicians and cherishing the biblical text. It also means asking questions of scripture and science alike. Our faith is always on the move and growing in light of new understandings of the world and humankind. Let us rejoice in our adventures with God to horizons currently unknown to us.

So What? This week's lectionary is a call to engage our faith holistically. Nothing is beyond examination or off the table in terms of *our* rituals, traditions, and doctrines. With Paul Tillich, we recognize that doubt is an essential aspect of faith. We can believe in God, as Madeleine L'Engle asserted, with all our doubts, recognizing that God is the receding horizon whose beauty and love constantly lures us forward.

This is a good Sunday to challenge misconceptions about Christianity with affirmations of the importance of science, technology, medicine, and the wisdom of other faith traditions. It also is an opportunity to remember that all of these, like our own religious concepts, are finite, relative, and subject to change. We can make the Bible an idol; we can also make science, medicine, and technology idols as well.

Roads Not Travelled. The adventurous preacher might explore themes such as "the appeal of atheism," "God loves science," "when science and scripture meet," "a scientist and a preacher go into a bar…," "doubting is good for your faith."

SPIRITUAL PRACTICES
FOR THE PREACHER AND CONGREGATION

Affirmative Faith. Today's affirmations invite us to embrace God's wisdom in all its dimensions.

I am open to truth and beauty wherever it is found.
Wherever there is truth and healing, God is its source.
My faith is growing as I encounter new understandings of the world.

Spiritual Practices for the Preacher. Today, let us live in God's light. Find a quiet place for prayer and meditation. Begin by breathing deeply and calmly. As you continue breathing, visualize a healing light entering you with every breath. Experience this light enlivening and enlightening you, and inspiring you, as your mind is bathed in divine light. Experience the light filling your whole body, with particular focus on your heart and hands. Experience your heart as filled with love and compassion for all creation; feel God's energy flowing from you to others in a healing way. Let every encounter today be an opportunity to bring life and light to the world.

Faith at home. This week's exercise follows the structure of "a spiritual practice for preachers." Children have vivid imaginations and can share in visually-inspired meditative practices.

Today, let us live in God's light. This may take a few more minutes as you convene your family for a time of group meditation Begin by breathing deeply and calmly. As you continue breathing, visualize a healing light entering you with every breath. Experience this light enlivening and enlightening you, and inspiring you, as your mind is bathed in light. Experience the light filling your whole body, with particular focus on your heart and hands. Experience your heart as filled with love and compassion for all creation; feel God's energy flowing from you to others in a healing way. Conclude with a conversation about how you can share the light of God in the world.

Twenty-Fourth Sunday after Pentecost
Mark 12:38-44

Once more, Jesus places himself at odds with the religious leaders. You need to walk the talk, Jesus proclaims. The author of the Letter of James put it another way: faith without works is dead. Let your life speak. Let your faith manifest itself in acts of love and compassion. Could Jesus' critique of the religious community, the community he loved and from whom he received many of his values, be related to those who call themselves Christians and indirectly harm others by closing factories and moving jobs overseas, foreclosing on homes, charging exorbitant interest rates, and laying off workers, noting it's only business and not personal? In the tradition of Jesus and the Hebraic prophets, everything is personal because everything shapes peoples' lives for good or ill.

Jesus turns his attention from the wealthy to the poor. An impoverished woman drops a penny in the temple offering. To the external observer, such a paltry gift is of little value. Jesus, however, notes that in contrast to the wealthy who give a small portion of her wealth, this woman gives everything. Her whole livelihood is at the disposal of God.

My depression era parents used to note that during the USA's most difficult economic times they still shared their resources with others. In their own words, "We weren't poor; we just didn't have any money." This woman has few of the world's resources, but she has a rich spirit. She is open to the needs of others and trusts that God will supply her deepest needs.

So What? Wealth and poverty are real; but they are also a matter of perception. Many wealthy people thirst for more money and power and end up on the wrong side of the law. They are indicted, tried, and sentenced for cheating on their taxes, taking the equivalent of a few dollars out of their vast fortunes. They are wealthy but they think small; they have everything except the feeling of abundant life. An impoverished woman leads to the way to freedom from consumption and acquisition. Her faith in God enables her to give away all she has. Despite her poverty, she is sharing in God's abundant life. She has everything she needs to live the good life.

114

SPIRITUAL PRACTICES
FOR THE PREACHER AND CONGREGATION

Affirmative Faith. We can experience abundant life in the midst of life's challenges, when we trust that God will supply our deepest needs.

> *God will supply my needs.*
> *I have all the time, money, and energy to live abundantly and*
> *do God's will.*
> *I give generously out of gratitude for God's gifts in my life.*

A Spiritual Practice for Preachers. In today's practice, we once again focus on God's energy enlivening and enlightening us. Begin your time of meditation with several gentle deep breaths. Then, experience divine energy flowing through you with each breath. Feel yourself filling up with divine energy from head to toe. In the experience of God's abundant life, experience this energy now flowing from you to others. Visualize certain persons in need of God's grace and see them being filled and surrounded by God's grace flowing in and through you.

Faith at Home. In addition to using the practice listed above in "a spiritual practice for preachers," take time to discuss the meaning and practice of generosity. What does it mean to be a good steward of time, talent, and treasure? How can we best use our resources and gifts to help others live abundantly?

Twenty-Fifth Sunday after Pentecost
Mark 13:1-8

All things must pass. The transitory nature of life is the one truth we must embrace, and often deny. Where is the Roman Empire today? Where is the global rule of Great Britain or the Ottoman Empire? In a blink of an eye, the infant grows into adulthood and a young adult is preparing for retirement and feeling the impact of the years. The Jerusalem Temple will be destroyed, and eventually so will the USA Capital, the Wall of China, and Egyptian Sphinx. The seas are rising near my home in Cape Cod, and perhaps in a thousand years much of Cape Cod will be reclaimed by the ocean. Perhaps a billion years from now gone will be the Grand Canyon, Rockies, and even planet earth. The future of humankind is at risk, most directly from our own behaviors.

We look for stability in a world of change. On this last week in our adventure with Mark, we embrace both change and constancy. Change is good. We want to grow up and our institutions need to evolve. Changelessness equals death in our world. But, change can be frightening especially when it threatens everything we love. We need change to grow and fulfill our dreams. We also yearn for something that abides, reminding us that in the perpetual perishing of life, there is something that lasts and that our lives will be treasured and remembered. This is the spirit of the hymn "Abide with Me," cited by the philosopher Alfred North Whitehead as a window into the relationship of God and the world.

> Abide with me; fast falls the eventide;
> The darkness deepens; Lord with me abide.
> When other helpers fail and comforts flee,
> Help of the helpless, O abide with me.
> Swift to its close ebbs out life's little day;
> Earth's joys grow dim; its glories pass away;
> Change and decay in all around I see;
> O Thou who changest not, abide with me.

God embraces all our changes, rejoicing in our celebrations and mourning in our sorrows. God is both the most changing and most changeless reality. God's faithfulness is great, God's mercies are new every morning.

Jesus warns of a time of false Messiahs, wars and rumors of war, nations at war with each other, and famines. We cannot identify any particular time with the coming of a new age, despite the proliferation of books on the Second Coming and a new Great Awakening. The expectation of dramatic transformation has characterized the human adventure, whether in the first or twenty-first centuries. Jesus notes that there will be birth pangs – labor pains - of this coming new age. Many of us feel that the womb of creation is laboring, and we wonder what will be born. We wonder if the future holds creation or destruction, and worry if the new birth for which we hope will be stillborn and our hopes for new creation dashed once more.

So What? Our hope amid all these challenges is the fidelity of God. God is here in all the changes of life and the divine midwife is bringing forth a future and hope for our world. Like the mustard seed, it grows slowly and silently. Like the five loaves and two fish, it seems insufficient to respond to today's demands. Mark knows, however, that once the seed is planted it will grow. The womb of the universe is in labor and will give birth to God's new creation when it is least expected. Have faith. God is faithful, and God's mercies are new every morning.

Roads Not Travelled. The adventurous preacher might preach on "Empires Lost" and challenge the congregation to ponder the eventual eclipse of the American empire and how we might creatively adjust to our own nation's descent. To move toward what some would call a more positive approach, the preacher might ask "What's being born in you?" Or "What must die for new life to be born?"

SPIRITUAL PRACTICES
FOR THE PREACHER AND CONGREGATION

Affirmative Faith. In the midst of constant transformation, we look for something that endures, not to deny change or decay, but to discover meaning and find inspiration to be agents of healing

> *God is my companion in the midst of change.*
> *God is faithful; God's mercies are new every morning.*
> *In life and death, God is with us.*

A Spiritual Practice for Preachers. We begin and end our journey in silence and beauty. After reflecting on Psalm 150:6, "let everything that breathes, praise God," take time to breathe in God's presence and celebrate the conclusion of your lectionary adventure with a walk in the autumn beauty.

117

Faith at Home. Autumn is harvest time. Take time this week to give thanks for the beauty of the earth. Share those things for which you are most thankful. Give thanks for God's faithfulness throughout all life's changes.

CHAPTER FOUR
THE ADVENTURE CONTINUES

There is an empty tomb and an open future. Mark's Jesus leaves the scene and is beyond our grasp. He is nowhere and everywhere. Like the adventurous paths Mark charts for the savior, Jesus is still on the move, now embodied in our cells and souls, and in everyday acts of healing, hospitality, and guidance. Jesus' good news enables us to turn from the ways of personal and corporate death toward new life and love. Jesus' good news invites us to simplicity and hospitality, to redefine power as relational, to see children and outcasts as God's beloved, to embrace healing and healers everywhere, and to discover that downward mobility leads to spiritual heights.

Mark's Jesus is on the move. We who have experienced the empty tomb are also on the move toward the open future and distant horizons toward which Jesus beckons. Like Mark, we preachers can share good news in novel ways, building on the stories of our community and the traditions of faith and leaning toward God's future. The tomb is empty and the pathway ahead is filled with possibility. Let the adventures continue!

CPSIA information can be obtained
at www.ICGtesting.com
Printed in the USA
FSHW020238110321
79229FS